Fireside Book of
North American Indian Folktales

Other books by the author

Indian Adventure Trails
Campfire and Council Ring Programs
Treasury of Memory-Making Campfires
Living Like Indians
Book of American Indian Games
Boy's Book of Indian Skills
American Indian Legends (The Limited Editions Club, N.Y.)
American Indian Legends (The Heritage Club, N.Y.)
Treasury of Memory-Making Indian Campfires
Modern Hunting With Indian Secrets

FIRESIDE BOOK
OF
NORTH AMERICAN
INDIAN
FOLKTALES

Legends and Lore of
Sea and Forest Trails, Trailcraft and Witchcraft,
Challenge and Contest, Warpaths and Warriors,
Powwows, Potlatches, Pueblos, Tepees and
Longhouses, Crests, Totems and Totem Poles, Ponies
and Paddles, Mystery, Medicine and Magic

by
Allan A. Macfarlan

Illustrations by
Paulette J. Macfarlan

STACKPOLE BOOKS

FIRESIDE BOOK OF NORTH AMERICAN INDIAN FOLKTALES

Copyright © 1974 by
ALLAN A. MACFARLAN

Published by
STACKPOLE BOOKS
Cameron and Kelker Streets
Harrisburg, Pa. 17105

Printed in the U.S.A.

Library of Congress Cataloging in Publication Data

Macfarlan, Allan A
    Fireside book of North American Indian folktales.

    SUMMARY: Presents a collection of traditional tales from various North American tribes under such headings as mystery and Magic, Romance and Enchantment, and Animal and Bird Folktales.
    1. Indians of North America--Legends. [1. Indians of North America--Legends] I. Macfarlan, Paulette Jumeau, illus. II. Title.
E98.F6M135   398.2'09701   74-19344
ISBN 0-8117-0635-4

Contents

6   Contents

MEDICINE MEN, TRANSFORMERS, TRICKSTERS, AND WITCHES

RAVEN TALES

ROMANCE AND ENCHANTMENT

MYSTERY AND MAGIC

ANIMAL AND BIRD FOLKTALES

8   *Contents*

HOW AND WHY TALES

UNDERSTANDING INDIAN WORDS AND PHRASES

INDEX OF TRIBES AND STORIES

Introduction

In order to enjoy these stories more, one should first know something about the Indian nations, tribes, and clans who people the tales and legends. Their greatly different ways of life are briefly described here.

The Indians of the Plains were known as buffalo hunters. They lived in tepees made of buffalo hide, and used it for robes, clothing, rawhide, shields, parfleches, and other things as well. They also hunted other game, and roamed the great plains, first on foot, later on horseback.

The Woodland Indians, dwellers in the woods and forests, were hunters who also did a little farming. They lived in longhouses built from logs and elm bark, often set between a strong framework of lashed poles. The roofs, which were slanted, were made from slabs of elm bark overlapping, like shingles. Big slits were left at the top, to let the smoke from the cooking fires escape. Many of these lodges were big enough to house twenty families or more. They used deer hide for

9

clothing, shields, and other things, and did beautiful quill and bead-work. These people made splendid canoes from birch bark, strong, lightweight craft ranging in size from two to ten-men canoes and even larger.

The Desert Dwellers of the Southwest were food-gatherers who also hunted. They usually lived in dwellings called hogans, which were built with poles and logs covered with earth. There was a big opening at the top of these earth lodges to let the smoke from the fire escape.

The Pueblo people, also known as the people of the mesas, farmed and hunted, wove splendid rugs, and made artistic jewelry. Their earliest homes were simple pit dwellings. Later they built houses into cliffs which had caves. They dug them out of the cliffs, taking advantage of cracks in the cliff walls, which made building easier. The holes and gaps in these two or three story houses were filled in with adobe, a clay which they later learned to make into sun-dried bricks. As their state of civilization advanced, they built huge, fantastic, cliff-canyon dwellings, some with more than 500 rooms; and with enormous *kivas* or chambers, many built underground, which were used by the men chiefly for religious ceremonials. As time went on, the Pueblo people built their cities out on the deserts and plains, on mesas, which are tablelands with steep sides. The dwellings, often of many stories, were very well built of stone, adobe bricks, or both.

Some of the Southern Indians, such as the Seminole, lived in a Chickee type dwelling, built on poles, with a thatched roof and a floor but no sides.

The Northwest Coast Indians were hardy people, known as

hunters of the sea or fishermen; some clans were called "hunters of whales." These people usually built their villages on big, sloping beaches, most often with a great cedar forest at the back of the village. Some of their houses were big enough to hold eight hundred people. These houses were beautifully built of strong, thick cedar planks, with a big roof section above the fire pit, which folded back to show the sky and allow the smoke to escape. Most of the painted and carved house fronts were further decorated by exterior posts which looked like short totem poles. In many villages, huge totem poles towered high into the air, giving the villages a fantastic and picturesque appearance. The totem poles were made from great cedar trees which were adorned with family crests and carved and painted with the figures of animals, birds, fish, and strange, mythical beings. Often, the figure of the chief who had the totem pole set up was carved and painted on the pole.

High on the beaches, canoes of all kinds were pulled up out of reach of the clutch of the tides. There were one-man craft, and big, sturdy whaling canoes, as well as the huge Haida war canoes which ranged from fifty to sixty feet in length and were able to carry from forty to fifty men. These superb canoes were splendidly carved and decorated with fantastic, upswept sterns and high bows. They were made from great cedar trees which were easy to work, burn out, steam, and shape. Planks were easily split from these cedars, and all of the cords and ropes needed were made from the tough fibers of these magnificent trees. So was clothing. The women also wove magnificent blankets from goat wool and soft hair from dogs.

These Northwest Coast Indians caught many tons of fish each

week to feed their clans. Great halibut and fish of many other kinds formed part of the daily catch; but the treasured fish of these Indians was the huge salmon. They were caught by the thousands when salmon season came around.

Story-Fire Tales

All folktales and legends of the many Indian nations, tribes, and clans, which inhabited the once vast Indian territories from the Atlantic to the Pacific coasts, have something in common. Hundreds of varied stories were woven by the skillful tellers of tales from old legends, myths, and many things which both old and young people sensed, knew, felt, and had experienced: the joy, sorrow, feasting, famine, and ecstasy of life. Many versions of these stories were told by the storytellers of the various tribes. Often, the backgrounds of the tales reflected the lure of adventure, the thrill of the chase, and the blood-chilling spells of mystery and magic. The weaver of the story webs also told vivid tales of the joy of achievement, the sting of defeat, the still and storm of lake and ocean, the fragrance of the forest, the excitement of spring, the sun of summer, and the woes of winter. Those who heard these tales knew that they were listening to an account of their way of life. Many tales told by the tribal storytellers inspired wonder, which in many cases developed into thought, causing those who listened around the story-fire to ask, "Why?"

Stories founded on old myths and legends were also the basis of many hundreds of tales, as were the long-past exploits of culture heroes. Even living Indians, who had legendary lives, became the source of hero worship.

Legends Today

Even today, a number of the figures in tribal legends are still regarded by the older modern Indians as being powerful and able to exert helpful influence, when called on to do so. The author of this book recently heard old Blackfoot women call on "Ghost Woman" to aid them in putting the long poles into the "ears" of the tepee covers— always a very difficult thing to do—when setting up these lodges on dark, windy nights.

Not only do older Indians make use of the legends of times long past, but the younger Indians also use such folktales to illustrate the uncertainty and strangeness of modern life.

Today, many old Indians of some tribes await the return of Glooscap, whom the reader will meet in these pages. Glooscap will come, his people believe, in his great stone canoe, manned by the Children of Light. Tricksters and transformers, such as Manabozho, though mocked by some modern American Indian youths, are still taken very seriously by others. Dream power, older people say, may come in the hours of sleep, and is still regarded as a potent factor in their lives.

Recently, the author saw some young Stoney Indian boys walk with their heads twisted to one side. They were hero worshippers, imitating the way in which Twist-in-the-Neck, the Stoney superman and culture hero, was supposed to have walked. He was the hero of many tales of the wonderful make-believe story land. The tales of this hero and his marvelous bull elk are reminiscent of Paul Bunyan and his blue ox, of American folktales. As with other folk heroes, the Indian storyteller often made this usually unbeatable hero get into difficult situations which made him appear ridiculous. The audiences were very fond of such stories.

Indian Storytellers

The folktales in this book were told by storytellers of the Plains, the Woodland people, the Desert Dwellers, and the Pueblo people of the Southwest, as well as the Indian clans of the Northwest Coast and islands. The storytellers of all these peoples were dynamic and dramatic; and, knowing the birds and animals intimately, they were able to imitate to perfection the whistles and calls of all the birds and animals in the territory, and bring them to life within the magic of the campfire circle.

The Indian storyteller built surprise and suspense into the framework of his tales, as he unwound them from his wonderful story store. He knew, as did his listeners, the characters which peopled his tales, so that they were seen reflected in the flickering flames of the story-fire. These storytellers could bring the fear and mystery of the darkest night into the brightness of the firelight. They thrilled their listeners and made the bravest chiefs glance fearfully over their shoulders at times, as strange, mysterious noises seemed to come from nowhere, and the presence of strange things was sensed without being seen.

The tales of the Indian storyteller were varied, and so they are in this book. Some are of high adventure, some tell of the wonders of nature, some tales are humorous, others tell of mystery and magic, while some are known as "how and why" stories, telling how and why the Indians came to believe in things as they were.

Medicine Men, Transformers, and Tricksters

Throughout all American Indian habitats, tribes had medicine men and medicine women, shamans and Wise Ones, whom the Indians believed possessed great powers. Some of them undoubtedly did. Indians went to these wise men to consult about the future and fate; others went to have individual, secret totems designed. Painted on a shield, for instance, the totem would make the enemy bowmen unable to injure the shield bearer. Medicine men provided secret talismans in the form of amulets, charms, decorations, and cords which, it was said, protected the bearers from evils and dangers, and assured good health and good hunting. The Indians believed that sickness was caused, often, by one or more evil spirits taking possession of their bodies; then it was the work of the medicine men or shamans to frighten the evil spirits out of the body which they had entered. The medicine men charged for their services, according to the condition of the patient and the nature of the cures needed. Sometimes the fee was very small: a skin or two or a pair of leggings, for advice or minor treatments. But for "big medicine," requiring much more effort and magic, the fee might be several horses, or more. Some of the more

superstitious Indians went to witches and sorcerers for advice and treatment, often with evil results.

Animal-People

Transformers, often tricksters too, were able to turn themselves into a bird or animal at will, and then change back into human form at will. Indian beliefs made little distinction between man and beast. A young man joined the deer, or a girl joined the bears, for example, taking on the characteristics of these animals. There was, supposedly, an interchangeability between humans and animals, so in many folktales men married deer or other animals, while women married animals of their choice; and happy marriages, so we are told, resulted from such strange alliances. There were strong taboos against offending an animal wife or husband, so animals were never scolded.

Manabozho, a transformer-trickster, used to address groups of humans and animals, "Ho! you animal-people!" In Indian texts, one reads many tales in which it is hard to know at first whether the story is about an adventurous person or an adventurous animal. For instance, "Manstin was an adventurous brave. . . ." A few paragraphs later one learns, chiefly by casual references to the hero's long, sensitive ears and quivering nose, that he is a rabbit!

Medicine, Magic, and Mystery

Practically everything which an Indian did not understand was a magic or mysterious thing which could be big, good, or bad medicine.

Such primitive beliefs gave birth to many beautiful legends of echoes, rainbows, and the like. Rainbows are mentioned in the legends of many tribes and were thought to possess great medicine power; in addition, in some tribal legends, the rainbow forms a bridge between the upper regions and earth. The stars moved by great magic. Striking nature oddities, such as a white buffalo, strangely formed animal horns, strange colors and crests of birds, and unusual flowers, were also considered mysterious, and often found a place in a folktale or legend.

Religion

The popular beliefs regarding the religion of American Indian tribes are, in general, as erroneous as those concerning the Indian way of life. The ideas of the "Great Spirit" and the "Happy Hunting Grounds" originated with the early missionaries, and were perpetuated by the public. The Indian words, from which the term Great Spirit was derived, actually had different meanings among different tribes. For instance, among the Dakota and Mandan Indians, the words mean "Great Medicine," and were used to describe anything mysterious which the Indians did not understand.

The tribes believed in many gods of varying prominence and power. The principal idea underlying the primitive religion of the Indians was to induce the gods to share the interests of man, and to inspire, pity, and help him. Countless activities in the Indian way of life were dedicated to these purposes. They communicated with their gods through elaborate ceremonies, including prayer, fasting, singing, chanting, dancing, and storytelling. There were religious festivals to invoke rain, good hunting, bountiful harvests, and good health. In various habitats, bear dances, buffalo dances, wolf dances, the dances of other animals, and bird dances, formed a part of religious ritual.

Fasting, to obtain powers of various sorts, was coupled with prayer as a means of communicating with deities and guardian spirits and as a part of secret worship. Both played a prominent part in the way of life of the North American Indians. Rich offerings were made to the various gods by powerful chiefs. Even the most humble members of the tribes made offerings, such as red paint, colored beads and pebbles, or even a few feathers.

The Thunderers, supernatural "above beings," were revered by some Plains tribes. The members carried their pipes with the stems upward, so that these deities could take a puff of the pipe more easily.

Many of the religious ceremonies were marked by sincerity and symbolism, among which the Iroquoian "Address of Thanksgiving to the Powers of the Master of Life" merits special mention.

Superstitions, Mystic Numbers, and Taboos

Superstitions played a large part in the thoughts, actions, and lives of the American Indians, and often altered their way of life. Signs, dreams, and unusual happenings were believed to bring good or bad fortune. The Indians believed that signs of good or ill omen were actually sent as warnings or as encouragement, by one of the supernatural beings. These beings made the path rough or smooth, for reasons which the Indians neither understood nor tried to fathom.

All American Indian tribes believed in the supernatural. They accepted spirits; dwarfs and elves, known as "The Little People"; water and land fairies; vampires; ghosts; monsters of many kinds; and mermaids and mermen. These beings often formed the themes of Indian folktales told around the story-fire.

The belief in the power of magic numbers was very strong. Medicine men and wise ones used them in cures and spells. In many tribes, four and seven were thought to be powerful, mystic numbers; and four times four, and seven times seven, were often regarded as sacred and most potent. The spirit power in these numbers was said to bring about the granting of wishes of almost every sort, effect cures, protect against evil spirits and ghosts, and assure special power and favors. The Indians held in awe great numbers, "many as the leaves on a big tree." For instance, no Teton dared to look at big star groups and count even one of them mentally, since he believed that once he had begun the count he must finish it or die.

Taboos were as many as the stars and had to be observed, in order to avoid misfortune or even death. There were taboos against telling certain stories at certain times: some tales could be told in the

daytime, but others must be told only after dark. Some games could be played only at certain times of year. There were taboos, at times, against wearing certain articles of clothing, and strong taboos against using a magic wish too often. A Cherokee was afraid to point at a rainbow with the index finger, because he believed that by doing so swelling and perhaps permanent injury would occur in the joints. It was quite all right, however, to point with the lips or elbows! Yawning was taboo among some tribes of the Northwest Coast, as it was believed that it attracted ghosts.

One could go on and on, on an almost endless trail of words, but story-time has come, and the teller of tales strides swiftly and silently into the story-fire circle, raises his hand in a salute to his listeners, and at once begins a folktale about the hardy, adventurous Indians who hunt, fish, adventure, laugh, and live in the pages of this book. . . .

Adventure, Misadventure, Daring and Peril

Thoughts on the Wind

Micmac

The Micmac storyteller raised his hand for silence and then told the story of the boy who, long ago, was saved from death by thoughts. Thoughts are very strong things, the storyteller explained, and you must believe in them and their power, or the magic of thought will not work for you.

A poor widow lived by the sea on the shore of what is now Eastern Canada. Her husband had been a fisherman, but he had been drowned when his canoe had been wrecked in a great storm, so now she lived alone with her son. Though he was still a young boy, he tried to fill the place of his father and had learned to be clever at fishing and hunting. What was just as important, he had learned not to fear the wild animals, stormy weather, and the cold of winter. The Great Eagle, feared by all of the people in that land, was the only thing which the boy feared. The huge bird was said to have magic power, and it had the power to make wind storms. Sometimes, when it was angry, it destroyed parts of the country by the winds which it caused by the strokes of its powerful wings.

Now, hunger came to the land and the people were starving. Even the best hunters found it hard to get game of any sort. Because he knew the ways of the animals better than the other hunters, the boy was able to find enough meat to take care of his and his mother's needs. One cold day, because he had trapped a fine, fat beaver at the door of its lodge, his great adventure began. He was carrying the beaver on his shoulder and was nearly home when he was attacked and carried off by the Great Eagle. The boy tried to wound the huge bird with a knife which he carried in his belt, but because of the grip of the eagle's talons in his shoulders, he was not able to cut through its thick feathers and only wounded the bird slightly.

The Great Eagle flew far until it reached its nest, which was on a high cliff overlooking the sea. There were young eagles in the nest crying loudly for food, and the boy knew that he would be fed to the young of the eagle as soon as they had eaten the big beaver which their mother had given them as soon as she reached the nest. The boy saw that it was impossible to escape from the high ledge. He could not reach the cliff beneath it, and the beach lay far below. Knowing that the boy could not get away, the Great Eagle left its nest to hunt for fish and game, but these were so scarce that it caught very few.

Back in her wigwam, the boy's mother thought that her son had been killed or drowned, and she wept all day long and often in the night. She was hungry, but her sorrow was far greater than her hunger. Soon, a very little woman came along and asked, "Why are you crying?"

The mother, who knew that the little old woman was one of the Little Folk of the Hills, told her about the boy. She told how the men of the tribe had searched for him in vain and said that he would never be found. Believing, as the people did, that the Little Folk had some magic powers which they used to help Indians in great difficulty, the poor mother told the little woman everything.

"In such a case, we can do nothing which will help to find your son," the little old woman said. "Only our thoughts will help. Fix your thoughts on your son, and he will see you or you will see him; and then my mind will tell you what to do to save him, if he is still alive." The old woman explained that thoughts were things, and the mother thought as hard as she could through the daylight and also when the sun had left to let the moon come.

When darkness came, the boy saw his mother very clearly in a dream. He explained his great danger to her, and the little old woman told the mother what thoughts to send him. She told the boy to shout loudly when he saw the eagle returning to the nest and to hold his knife strongly, with the handle placed firmly on the rock, point upward, so the bird would kill itself when it swooped down on the boy from the air.

The boy, who did not know about the power of thought, did nothing for two days and nights and did not even try to reach his mother by thought. Because of this, she could not make her thoughts-on-the-wind reach him. At last, he had to follow the advice of his mother because, as darkness was about to come on the second day, the eaglets had eaten all of the beaver and the few fish and rabbits which their mother had brought them, and the boy felt sure that when the mother bird returned to the nest she would tear him up and feed him to her young. The boy prepared for the return of the Great Eagle by lying close to the nest, with the hilt of the keen knife held on the rock behind him. Soon, he saw a speck in the darkening sky and quickly the eagle swooped downward. The boy shouted shrilly and the eagle struck. As its breast struck the body of the young hunter, the force of the dive drove the knife into the bird's body so that it died almost at once.

Still the boy did not know what to do since he was still a prisoner on the ledge. He ate a young eagle, to give him strength, lay down on the Great Eagle because it was softer than lying on the hard rock, and thought hard about his mother, so that his thoughts would reach her. They did; and she scolded him because she was very angry and feared that the thoughts which she would send, with the help of the little old woman, would be too late to save him. "Listen," she commanded, and the boy did listen. Then his mother gave him a magic message from the old woman of the Little Folk of the Hills. She explained how to skin the eagle so that its skin and feathers would not be damaged. Its feet and head must not be injured and must be left on the skin.

The boy did what the thought-directions of his mother had told him, and soon the eagle skin was ready and lay before him like a great feather cloak. He was told that when the sun came, he was to dress himself in the cloak, and power would be given him to fly from the top of the cliff to the beach far below. When the time came, the boy stepped into the eagle skin, put his arms up inside the wings, and like a giant bird glided down onto the edge of the beach where the ocean rippled in and licked the talons on its feet. Up on the beach, he tried to fly but the wings would not carry him. He was sad because of this. He would have liked to fly back to his home and be greeted with admiring shouts from the people of the village. Instead, he had to find his way over a long and very difficult path, until at last he reached his wigwam and his happy mother.

For a while, he seemed so much astonished at his great adventure that he spoke very little about it; but after a while he began to boast about the wonderful, perhaps magic thing which had happened to him. As he boasted of his bravery and cleverness, he began to lose his skill as a hunter. Soon, he brought home so little game that he was forced to ask other hunters of his village to give him and his mother some of the game which they brought back from the chase, because they had no meat in the wigwam.

The poor mother, who did not like the boasting of her son nor accepting food from other hunters, sent a thought-message to the little old woman, who quickly came to help the mother in her trouble. She scolded the boy and called him a "boaster," and "a foolish, lazy one." She told him angrily, "Your strength and hunting skill were powerless to help you without our thoughts," and she warned him that unless he changed his ways he would lose all of his skill as a woodsman and hunter, and the people of his village would laugh at him and refuse to help.

The little old woman suddenly disappeared while the boy was looking at her, so he feared her magic and made up his mind to change his way of life as the woman had told him to do. He ceased to boast and soon became, once again, a great hunter.

✳ ✳ ✳

The Giant Crab of Chief Rock
Haida

The Haida storyteller tells the story in this way.

In the harbor of Naden stood the small but important island called Chief Rock, after the great chief whose huge house stood on the pine-clad rock. A giant crab lived at the mouth of the harbor to stop enemies and let pass the chief's friends. The chief decided to give a great potlatch to celebrate the raising of a great totem pole to honor his family. There would be much gift-giving and the chief invited many of his friends, including the Whale Killers from Rose Spit.

As their slave crews paddled their great canoes into the harbor, the Whale Killers saw pillars of smoke rising high into the air above the house of Chief Rock. The chiefs made jokes about the fire, and some said that he was burning down his house to avoid giving so many great gifts to the visiting friends. One of the servants of Chief Rock had gone out with a party to meet the visitors. When he overheard the unpleasant jibes of the Whale Killers, he paddled back to tell his master. Perhaps, thought Chief Rock, these Whale Killers come as enemies, rather than friends. At once, he ordered his warriors and his many different sorts of servants, among which was the huge crab, to attack and destroy the Whale Killers.

The great crab at once blocked the entry to the harbor and the Whale Killers, who saw the great war canoes setting off from the island, attacked the crab guardian in order to escape to the ocean. The crab crushed the canoes and killed most of the Whale Killers. They fought bravely, but neither their spears nor knives could pierce the armor of the shell of the fierce crab. Only a few of the Whale Killers escaped along the shore to safety.

Tales of the great power of the unbeatable crab soon spread among the islands. The Eagle Clan, which was nearest to the Chief Rock island, fled from their Skidegate village. In the speed of their

flight, they left behind an old woman and her grandson and his sister, who were unable to paddle far enough to join a friendly clan. As time passed, the boy grew to be big and strong and helped his grandmother and small sister to find enough food to live on, but their life was a hard one. They lived on shellfish, small fish which he could catch from a little raft, and some small birds and animals which he was able to shoot with the arrows from a bow which he had made. Nobody dared return to the deserted village.

One morning, the boy saw high in the blue sky a great eagle flying toward him. As its great wing strokes carried the bird nearer, the boy saw that it carried a big, shining thing in its strong talons. As the eagle flew low over the boy, it dropped a big halibut onto the sand. Happily, the boy dragged the big fish to his grandmother. She was joyful at getting such fine food.

The old woman was about to cut off a piece of the halibut's tail with her sharp knife, when all around her she heard noises of protest.

The trees swayed and sighed, rocks rolled and crashed into each other, and great waves rose from a still sea. Since she and the children needed food badly, she was about to cut off the head of the fish, when once again she was alarmed by the loud sounds of protest.

"Magic must be in this fish," she told her grandson, "and I must prepare it with great care." Then she began to skin the fish carefully, and this time there were no sounds of protest; so she skinned the halibut with very great care, assuring it as she worked that she was greatly favored by being able to skin such a splendid fish. She left the tail and head on the skin and then hung it carefully on the branch of a tree to dry.

When the skin was dry, the boy felt a great desire to play at being a fish, so he took down the skin and slipped into it. To his great surprise, the skin was soft and strong, and it fit him very well. He felt so pleased and fish-like that he slipped into the ocean where, helped by some strange power, he swam far out and then around the islands for a day and a night. He did not feel tired as he slid up on shore, when he returned home, and slipped out of the fish skin. His grandmother and sister welcomed his return and did not scold him for the fright he had given them by his daring and long absence. The boy was surprised that his grandmother did not question him about why he had done what he did nor ask about his voyage. She must know that much magic lies in the skin, he thought.

Each day he went swimming and one day when he swam close to the big rock, at what is now Dawson Harbor, it talked to him. "You are now big and strong and without fear," it told him, "so you must now go and kill the savage crab of Naden Harbor."

Without asking a question, the boy glided swiftly away. He swam around the west coast until at last he saw the giant crab guarding the entrance to the harbor. He knew that the claws of the huge crab could tear him to pieces if he tried to approach it from in front, so he dived deep into the ocean and came up behind the crab. He attacked it from directly behind and bit into it where its armor was softest. He bit deeper and deeper into the crab as it tried desperately to shake him off, and after a big fight the boy killed the crab.

After resting for a long while, the boy tore the crab apart and then chewed it into pieces and spat them into the water of the harbor. "May each piece become a little crab, and each little crab become a big crab, and so become food for my people," he said. And so it was.

✳   ✳   ✳

The Sharp-Nosed One

Tsimshian

In a Tsimshian village, the great winter ceremonies held the older
people in their grip. They had neither time nor thought for other
things. Outside of the village, a band of older children, who were still
not old enough to attend the ceremonies, played at being grownups.
They were holding their own ceremonies of winter. They had built a
big house of branches and were singing, shouting and dancing from
the time when the sun came until it left to let the moon come. Even
then they still danced to the rhythm of skin drums. The noise they
made kept the forest awake because there were no thick cedar planks
to shut it inside their roughly built house.

    The great noise which the children made trailed skyward with the
smoke from their fires and the Sky Chief could not sleep. He was
angry and sent one of his slaves down to see what was taking place.
"Tell those earth people that they must cease their noise making or I
will use my magic to make it cease. Go!" he ordered.

    The slave obeyed. He spoke with the noise makers and warned
them that something terrible might happen to all of them if the noise

did not stop. The children saw that the strange man who spoke to them was a slave, and they paid no heed to his words.

The slave returned and told the Sky Chief that the noisy children played at "Potlatch." He had told them, he said, that the noise must stop at once.

"Good," replied the Sky Chief, "but they have not obeyed. Their shouts still disturb me. If the noise keeps on when darkness comes, take helpers and bring all of the noise makers here. I have spoken."

The noise continued so the slaves of the Sky Chief went down to do as their master had ordered. When they reached the big house of branches, all of the children were tired out and slept soundly.

"Better for them had they slept much sooner," said a slave as they took the children, the house, and the ground on which it stood up into the Land of the Sky.

When the children awakened, a boy looked out through the doorway of the house. What he saw made him fear greatly. "There is something wrong here!" he called to the others. All awoke at his shout. As they did so, the slave who had warned them stood just outside the door of their house. Behind him stood a giant. Some of the bigger boys tried to run away but they were seized by the long-armed giant who threw them back into the house.

"You did not obey as children should," the slave told them. "You made much noise after I left. My master could not sleep. Now you will be punished for your noise making."

The slave picked up the biggest boy as though he were a rabbit and carried him, though the boy struggled and fought, to the back door of a great house which stood nearby. "I have one of the makers of noise outside, master," he called.

The Sky Chief was thinking of a way to punish those who had disturbed him when loud shrieks of terror from the other children made him frown darkly. "Take the one you have brought me to the front!" he commanded angrily.

The slave took the boy to the front of the house where a great, glistening totem pole stood. A huge, shining figure on the pole looked as though it were alive. It had a long, sharp nose like the beak of a hawk. The slave stood the frightened boy in front of the pole. The boy cried loudly but he was too afraid to move. Suddenly, the keen, cutting nose of the figure on the pole sliced the boy into two pieces. Women came and took the two halves away.

When the boy's cries had ceased and he was not taken back to the house, the children were even more frightened than before. They wept and screamed in their terror. The noise was frightful. Only one girl did not cry. "I am a princess," she said proudly, "and princesses do not cry."

Sky Chief, who was trying to go to sleep, was furious when he heard the new outcry. "Take another noise-making child to the front," he shouted to his slave. "Tell the others that all who cry will be taken one by one until no more noise do I hear."

The slave went to the guarded children. "Another do I take," he said. "One by one, those who cry shall look upon the magic totem pole of my master. It is his command." He picked up a big girl and carried her screaming to the sharp-nosed pole. Soon her screams ceased and the slave came for another crying child.

"Why do you not take me, slave?" asked the dry-eyed princess. "I fear not your master nor his magic totem pole." She spoke clearly and loudly and the slave's face became white with fear.

"Speak not so, princess," he begged as he picked up another boy and hurried out. Soon only one child was left, the princess who was too proud to weep.

When the slave told his master that he was about to take the last child, a girl, to the front, the Sky Chief said, "Strange, I do not hear her cry."

"No, Chief," said the slave, "she is a princess and she is very brave."

The Sky Chief had a thought but he sent it from his mind because he was still very angry from loss of sleep. "No, I will make an end to all of those noise makers," he decided. "Take her to the front!"

The slave felt very sorry for the princess but he dared not disobey the order. "I have been sent for you, princess," he said sadly, when he went to get her.

She was braiding her hair. "I must wash and fix my clothes first, then will I come, slave." Soon she stood at the door of the house of branches. She wore a robe of sea otter skins and looked calm and fearless.

Sorrowfully the slave led her out in front of the sharp-nosed one. The princess stood up very straight in front of the monster. She gazed into its cold, fish-like eyes which stared cruelly. The sharp nose rose, then fell, quick as a lightning flash. It slashed through the robe of sea otter then shattered with a loud splintering sound into many pieces. The noise of its breaking sounded like the falling of many small icicles from a great height. The princess stood unharmed.

Sky Chief strode swiftly from his house to see what had happened. One quick glance told him. "Come my brave daughter," he said kindly, stretching out his hand to the young princess. He took her into his huge house and seated her on rich furs beside him. "You have great courage, princess. You know not fear. You shall marry my son."

"Only if he is of royal blood and I find that I love him," she replied firmly.

Sky Chief laughed loudly and looked at her in wonder. He called for his son.

A tall, handsome young man came into the room. The princess liked him very well at the first glance. Sky Chief ordered a great feast and after they had finished feasting a shaman married the young people. Their lives were very happy but at times the princess thought of her people and was sad. In time, a baby boy was born. He was big and did not cry like other babies. Sky Chief was very fond of the child and his heart was heavy when one day the princess asked to return to earth with her husband and child.

"Although I am happy here, I am lonely for my people and they may need me," she said.

Sky Chief knew that he would miss his children but he wished the princess to be happy and he knew that his son wished to visit the earth people. "You may return to your people," he told the princess. Soon they were ready for the journey.

The young chief covered the head of his wife with a soft blanket. "It is not well that you see how we go," he told her.

She held her baby tightly as she felt the air rushing past. The arms of her husband held her close. Soon she felt ground beneath her feet. The blanket was taken from her head and she saw that she stood in front of the great house of her uncle.

People shouted and the uncle came to the door. He looked much older than when she last saw him. He did not know who the beautiful young woman was who stood outside.

The princess sang a personal song of her family. Then her uncle and the people knew who she was and welcomed her and also her husband and child. In the house of her uncle she told her relatives and chiefs the story of her stay with Sky Chief and of her marriage to his son.

Her uncle gave a great name-giving potlatch. After much feasting and rejoicing he took his speaker's staff in hand and spoke to his guests. "I grow old and now give my nephew my name and place as prince and chief. The sharp-cutting-nosed one, of which you have heard the story, shall be his crest and that of his descendents. I have spoken."

* * *

The Bridge of Ice
Tsimshian

The Tsimshian Chief-Who-Doubted had done a bad thing. He had quarreled with an old Wise One and, in the fight that followed, had killed him. This started a feud which made many enemies for the tribe of the Chief-Who-Doubted. The foes, on the other side of the Stikine River, were far too many for the small band of the chief to fight.

Safety lay in flight, the Chief-Who-Doubted and his counselors decided. They fled down the swift-flowing river in six big canoes, singing dirges as they went. The fast current of the wide stream saved them from swift pursuit, and things went well with the little band until they saw a great barrier of ice blocking the river ahead of them.

Flight could only be continued by canoe, so the Chief-Who-Doubted landed on the bank of the stream with some of his counselors, to see what could be done. One of the keen-eyed counselors thought that he could see the foaming water flowing under the glistening ice barrier. There seemed to be a tunnel running below the great wall of ice, but it was not possible to tell how wide or how high it was.

The Chief-Who-Doubted decided on a way to find out if he and his band could pass safely under the bridge of ice, in their great canoes. He sent some of his men along the bank to watch on the far side of the barrier while others cut down a cottonwood tree, so that it fell into the river. They did not chop off the branches and the tree was whirled downstream by the rushing water. Those in the canoes lost sight of the tree when it reached the ice wall, but those with the keenest eyes thought that they saw it disappear underneath, toward the middle of the stream. When the men returned from the other side of the barrier, they told the chief that they had watched a big cottonwood pass safely under the barrier with its branches unbroken.

"The tree, wearing its branches, passed under safely," said the chief. "So can we." He sat in the bow of the first of the six canoes. He wore his big conical hat, which towered high above his head. The paddlers drove the canoe out into the rushing current and, followed by the other canoes, headed for the patch of foaming water which showed white in the barrier of blue ice.

As they came closer, they saw that the canoes were being drawn into what looked like the entrance to a great, dark cave. The paddlers urged the canoes forward, aiming directly for the center of the opening. For what seemed a long time, they rushed forward in greenish darkness; then, like arrows shot from strong bows, they flashed out into the bright sunlight.

They continued their voyage until they reached salt water in the river, and then the ocean lay before them. Today, a tall conical hat, like the one worn by the Chief-Who-Doubted, may be seen on the top of some totem poles. They were carved in remembrance of the dangerous voyage through the bridge of ice.

✳ ✳ ✳

Thunder Falls

Kickapoo

The blanket of night had wrapped the Kickapoo village in darkness. The people were gathered around the story-fire, awaiting the tale which the storyteller would tell. The listeners knew that the tale would not be of braves on the war trail, nor warriors who risked their lives on raids into the country of their enemies. And yet, the story which they were about to hear was one of high courage. It was of two brave women who were still honored in song and dance, because of their great courage and their noble sacrifice made for their tribe. This is the story that the people heard.

A band of our men were hunting, when the green earth had come from beneath the snow, and rivers were fat and fast. Women were with the men, to help skin the animals taken in the chase, and to strip and dry the meat. For three suns the party had hunted, and deer had fallen to their hunting arrows.

As they traveled in country distant from our territory, there was always danger of attack by enemies. Braves kept watch always, but they did not watch well enough. One day, the chief said it would be a good thing to return to the tribe, and the party made ready to go back when the sun came. Some of the braves and women did not see the sun again. A big war party of Shawnee surrounded and attacked the camp, when night was leaving to let morning come.

The Kickapoo who were not killed or badly wounded escaped down into the gorges. They had hunted there and found a great cave, beneath the thundering falls of a mighty river. The chief had decided that they would hide there, if they saw a large war party of the enemy, so all of the Kickapoo knew the hiding place.

The savage Shawnee killed the wounded, and took two of our women back to their camp, as prisoners. The women were young and would be made to work. The camp of the Shawnee was far above the place where they had attacked our party. Their lodges were on the banks of the wide, fast-flowing river.

For six suns after the attack, the Shawnee warriors searched for our people who had escaped the raid. Sentries were placed at distant points, so that the Kickapoo could not escape without being seen. The big war party of the Shawnee would be told of their movements. The enemy searched well, but our people hid better and were not discovered. Our chief did not let his party leave the great cavern, nor did they need to, for they had dried meat and water in plenty.

After some suns had passed, the people begged the chief to let them leave the shelter of the big cave beneath the falls. They felt safe there, but the terrible noise of the falls hurt their ears, as it roared like a curtain of thunder before the cavern. Their minds were afraid too, for they feared that spirits of evil dwelt in the dark, rocky gorges which surrounded them.

The chief was brave, but he knew how his band felt. He too would be happy to leave the great roaring and rumbling far behind him, even if, in escaping, more of his band would fall to the arrows of the Shawnee. "Tomorrow, the day of the seventh sun since the attack, will be the last that we remain here," he told his band. "When darkness comes, we will try to escape from the enemy into our own territory. Be ready!"

Our chief knew that the chances of reaching safety were few, as the Shawnee were many and must be angry that any of our people had escaped the raid. "Their anger must be very great," the Kickapoo chief thought, "because though they could follow the trails in the forest, their best trailers could not see footprints on the rocky ground which formed the river gorges."

The medicine man of the Shawnee went to their chief on the morning of the seventh sun, and told him of a dream which he had had. His totem bird, the red-tailed hawk, had come to him in a dream and flown around and around him in circles, giving shrill cries and tempting him to follow it. The medicine man could not refuse to follow his totem bird, so his spirit followed it, as it flew swiftly before him, until the hawk reached a clearing in the forest. Here, in the dream, the medicine man saw a circle of Shadow People.

"Can I follow the Shadow People to where our enemies are hidden?" the medicine man asked the hawk. "Who among them knows where the band is hiding?"

The hawk flew straight to the two women who were the prisoners of the Shawnee and circled the head of each.

"These women must know," declared the medicine man, as he told his chief of the dream. "My hawk totem never leads me on a false trail."

The Shawnee chief had great faith in the medicine man and his totem bird; so he called a council of his warriors. He told them of the dream and had the two captive women brought before him. When

questioned, they declared that they did not know where the band to which they had belonged was hidden.

"They speak with a crooked tongue," shouted the medicine man, "but torture will make it straight."

The women were tortured, and under the bite of blazing twigs held to their wrists, they cried out that they would reveal the hiding place of their band. For a moment, they spoke softly together in their own dialect and then, by signs, showed that they were ready to lead the Shawnee war party to the hiding place.

When the Shawnee were armed, and about to follow them, the two women pointed to the river, instead of leading the way into the forest. By signs, they showed that our people were far away and could be reached quicker by the Shawnees if they went by canoe. When the chief pointed toward the forest and his braves pushed the women in that direction, they showed by sign talk that they could not lead the Shawnees by land. Only by water did they know the way to the hidden Kickapoo band.

The chief believed the women, and they were taken to the big canoes that lay on the river bank. With hands and sounds, the women told that close to the falls there was a little branch of the main river, which they must follow to reach the Kickapoo. The chief ordered the women into the leading canoe. He too sat in it, with his medicine man and six of his best warriors. The rest of the party followed close behind, in many canoes. Paddles flashed and the canoes went swift as a fish downstream.

After paddling far, the chief asked the women if they were not yet near the hiding place of his enemies. The women sign-talked that the place was near, and again the paddles rose and fell. The braves did not have to paddle so hard now, because the current was becoming swifter and stronger, as the canoes sped along. Quicker and quicker the canoes traveled. From the distance came the thunder of the falls. Closer and closer came the earth-shaking roar.

The chief was brave, but even he feared the mighty force of the swift-rushing waters. He was directly behind the two captive women, who sat in the bow. He touched them on the shoulders, and they turned to him at once. The chief ceased to fear when he saw that both women were smiling. The elder of the two with a wave of her arm toward the south bank, showed that in a moment they would reach the fork of the river, where the paddlers could swing the canoes from the rushing current into the calm water of the smaller stream.

Faster, ever faster, the canoes now dashed through the foaming torrent. Narrower grew the rushing river as it roared between solid walls of rock. No time to try to turn the canoes!

Too late, the chief and warriors knew that they had been tricked. The bravest had but time to sing a few notes of their death songs before the raging torrent swept the shattered canoes over the crest of the mighty waterfall. Proudly leading the band of enemy warriors to death on the jagged rocks below were the two brave women of the Kickapoo.

My story is done, but that of the two who saved our band of warriors from death will go on as long as grass grows and water runs.

* * *

The Eagle Chief Swoops
Haida

A young Haida chief without fear died in a great battle in which many warriors fought against him. Good spirits took him to the spirit land of the eagles, high above the Queen Charlotte Islands. The old eagle chief who was the oldest in the spirit land greeted him as a brother and all the other eagle warriors were glad to have the young warrior with them. They gave him the wings of eagles and soon he learned to fly strongly, fearlessly, and far.

At night, when they gathered around the council fire, the old eagle chief liked to tell of his many adventures. When he told of his fierce fight with great whales and how he had won through his strength and skill, only the young warrior believed him. The young eagle warriors thought that his age made the old chief boast and weave stories from his imagination.

Encouraged by the stories of the old eagle chief, the young brave decided to fly over the ocean in search of a whale and fight it all by himself. When the sun came, he put on his eagle feathers and flew out to sea. He saw some whales with dorsal fins but he was afraid of them because the old chief had said that even he had never dared to fight a killer whale. Other whales the young chief saw, but they were so big he knew that even if he killed one in battle, he could not carry it back in his talons as proof of his victory.

When the young chief was about to fly back to the spirit land of the eagles, because the sun was leaving to make room for darkness, he saw a whale in the ocean, almost underneath him. It had no dorsal fin and was about ten times as long as a tall man was high. Eager for battle, the young chief dived swiftly onto the whale and dug his sharp talons far into its back. Beating his wings strongly, the young chief tried to fly upward but could not. The whale did not seem to know that someone was trying to lift it from the water. When the young chief could neither move the whale nor release his talons from its body, he was afraid and gave the loud cry of an eagle in distress.

The loud *Kre-e-e-e-e-s* were heard by distant eagle warriors who took up the cry as they flew to the rescue. They had all vowed to help each other in time of danger, so each one set out from wherever he was, to help the brother in need. When they reached the young chief, they dived one by one onto the great whale. Some of them drove their talons into the beast, while others tried to pull the young warrior from the whale's back.

The effects of the attacks at last seemed to be noticed by the whale. It started to dive. Then from high overhead the eagle warriors heard a shrill, terrible scream of an eagle, such as they had never heard before. It was the old eagle chief who had heard the cries for help and knew that the young eagle warriors were in danger. When he was directly overhead, he dived swiftly toward the whale, which was fast disappearing under the waves, dragging the young chief and the eagle warriors with it. With the speed of an arrow shot from a strong bow, the eagle chief dropped. He thrust his long, powerful talons deep into the back of the whale, which was already under water.

With mighty wing beats, the old eagle chief slowly lifted the great whale into the air and flew off toward the spirit land of the eagles with the huge beast held fast in his talons. The young chief and the warriors knew that had the old chief not rescued them, they would have been dragged down to the spirit world beneath the ocean. They were very grateful to the old chief and those who had doubted his stories were ashamed. All of them planned to honor him at a great naming ceremony.

The ceremony was held at a great council fire. They begged the old chief to tell them stories of his fights wih other whales, to which they listened with wonder and belief. Then they gave the old chief his new name, Mightier-than-the-Whales.

Today, one may see carved figures of the great eagle perched on the place of honor on top of many towering totem poles.

* * *

Stronger Than the North Wind

Tlingit

Only the bravest and strongest of the Tlingit hunters dared to hunt the sea lion. Arrows and spears were but poor weapons to use against such huge, strong creatures. One day, during the fierce battle between hunters of the Tlingit and sea lions, on Sea Lion Rock, a chief was killed by one stroke from the flailing tail of the biggest of the beasts.

"We go now," shouted the hunters as they carried the dead man to their canoes, "but the nephews of the chief whom you have killed will come back for revenge. They will tear you in two with their bare hands."

When the two nephews heard of the boast, which the hunters also regarded as a promise, their hearts were heavy. They wanted to avenge the death of their uncle, but the thought of killing an animal so huge, powerful, and fierce when aroused, even with a spear, put fear into their hearts. To kill the sea lion leader with their bare hands was much worse, but they would not lose face by killing the beast in any other way than the one that had been vowed by the hunters.

For a while, the nephews thought and did nothing. To encourage them, all of the strong men of the village started to train for battle. The nephews, who were also very strong, started to train too. All of these men hardened themselves by bathing in the ice cold streams and the cold ocean, while the winter winds blew on their naked bodies. They twisted strong tree branches and hurled big rocks into the ocean, to strengthen their hands and arms.

When they felt nearly strong enough for their fight with the sea lions, they planned tests which would show whether they were really ready for battle or only thought they were. There was a strong, tough spruce tree just outside the village. It was almost twice as tall as a man. One test was to see who would be first to bend the tree over and twist it right down to its roots. There was also a great dead tree with a thick branch which a man could just reach from the ground. The second test was to pull this big limb out of the trunk. At the end of three moons, none had done either of these things.

In the village lived a humble man about whom the others knew very little. He too was a nephew of the chief who had been killed by the sea lion and he too wanted to avenge his uncle's death. He told nobody except his aunt of his intentions because he was looked down on as a weak and lazy man. The men of the village thought that he did not bathe and exercise enough. They had forgotten that he was a nephew of the dead chief. They called him Dirty One.

Only the wife of his dead uncle knew how hard he was training for the fight with the sea lion leader. The other men did not know what he did because he ran and threw rocks and wrestled with young trees during the night while the others slept. He bathed and swam for so long in the ocean that he was glad to sleep in the warm ashes of the fire after he had crawled from the freezing water. This made him look dirtier than ever and the men laughed at him.

One night, while he sat in the ocean, a little man suddenly appeared on the beach and beckoned him to come on shore. The young man went up onto the beach and the little man said, "I look small, but I am called Strength of the North Wind. Wrestle with me."

The nephew closed with the stranger and they wrestled for a while, a very little while, because Strength of the North Wind threw the young man over his head. "You are not ready yet," the stranger told him, "nor is it the time for you to try to pull the branch out of the tree nor twist the strength-test-tree. When you are stronger, I will see you again," the little man promised. Then he was gone.

The new moon had come when the little man appeared on the beach again. The nephew, who was throwing boulders into the ocean, felt the stranger's eyes on him, and rushed toward him. They wrestled, and now it was the nephew who won.

"Now you are ready," Strength of the North Wind told him. "Go and pull out the big branch and twist the test tree."

Eagerly, the young man ran to the tree and easily pulled the limb from the trunk.

"Put the branch back," Strength commanded.

The nephew could not do so at first, because the branch would not stay in place. Then he spat in the hole from which he had pulled the branch, and the limb stayed in place.

"Now, the test tree," said Strength of the North Wind.

The young man ran to the spruce, seized it, and twisted it far down into the roots.

"Now you are ready to fight the sea lion," Strength of the North Wind declared. "You are as strong as I, and no other man is as strong."

When the sun came again, the two other nephews and the strong men of the village went to the test tree. The older brother twisted it out by the roots and the others thought that he was ready. When they reached the tree with the test branch, the younger brother was given first chance. He easily pulled the branch from the tree.

"Now you are both ready to do battle with the sea lions," the older men told the two nephews. They chose the strongest men in the party to go with them and went down to the beach to set out at once for Sea Lion Rock.

The other nephew had been watching. He ran to his aunt. "Give me the weasel-skin hat of my uncle," he begged. "I am ready for the challenge and will go with the others."

Wearing the hat, he ran down to the beach and, to the great surprise of the warriors in the big canoe, asked to be taken along.

They laughed at him and would have pushed him away with their paddles but he stood his ground. He seized the stern of the canoe so that they could not paddle away. They were too eager to start for Sea Lion Rock to notice how strong he must be to hold the big canoe against the strong strokes of six paddlers.

At last, since he too was a nephew of the dead chief, they took him along to bail out the canoe when it shipped water from the great waves.

With great difficulty, they reached the rock and held the canoe steady in the giant waves while the older brother managed to jump onto the rock. The sea lions rallied to defend their lives and their home. The brother rushed among them, cracking their heads open on the jagged rocks. Always he pushed toward the big bull sea lion which he knew had killed his uncle. At last he reached it, seized it by the tail, and tried to tear it in two. It was far stronger than he and with one stroke of its mighty flipper crushed the man flat on the rocks. By that time, the second nephew was on the rock. He rushed toward the bull. It killed him with one terrible stroke of its tail.

In great fear, the other men would have paddled swiftly away from the rock but the remaining nephew cried, "Stop! It was I who first pulled the branch from the tree and twisted the spruce. That is why it was easy for the others. I too have trained hard for this battle and I too am a nephew of the chief whom I have come to avenge. See, I wear his hat and am ready!"

The men paddled closer to the rock. The nephew rushed to the bow of the canoe, balanced for a heartbeat, then jumped safely onto the rock. He pushed the smaller sea lions aside. When they tried to fight, he swung them over his head by their tails, cracking their skulls open on the rocks. Two smaller bulls rushed him but he tossed them over his head into the ocean. The sea lion leader turned toward him. The nephew dodged behind it, seized it by the tail and tore it in two. Thus was the death of his uncle avenged in the blood of the great bull which had killed him. The Strong One, as the surprised men in the canoe now called him, was taken back to the village in triumph and soon became the town chief.

Today, the great carved interior posts of a house of the Tlingit tell how Strong One, a chief and warrior of the Raven clan, tore a great sea lion in two with his bare hands.

✳   ✳   ✳

Crests, Totems, Totem Poles, and Potlatches

Crest From the Ocean

Tsimshian

A Tsimshian fisherman who had fished for three suns without catching a fish was very sad. He prayed to the ocean people, as he pulled up his anchor of stone, to seek a new place to fish, and asked that good fortune might favor him.

He paddled to where the foot of a high mountain disappeared under the water, at the edge of the ocean. There he let his heavy anchor drop over the side of his dugout canoe. He did not know that it dropped with a loud noise onto the roof of a house of a killer whale, the most powerful of all the ocean people. When the killer whale heard the noise on his roof, he went out to see what had happened. Then he took hold of the anchor rope and pulled the canoe and fisherman into the house.

The fisherman was afraid. He expected to be killed or made a slave. This did not happen. Killer Whale wanted the Indians to use him as a totem crest, and so he treated the fisherman as an honored guest. For many moons, the killer whale taught the man how to draw and paint figures of the killer whale. He also showed the fisherman how to dance the dance of the killer whale and make masks and headdresses of the killer whale. When the man had learned to do these things well, Killer Whale put him into his canoe and took him up to the surface of the ocean.

The fisherman thought that he had not been gone for more than one moon, until he saw his house! It had been nearly destroyed by the ocean. All that was left was a seaweed-covered framework. He built a new house and painted a killer whale on its front. Then he painted a killer whale on a dance blanket, and made a dance mask in the shape of a killer whale. He beat the invitation drum and people came from the village. He astonished them by doing the dance of the killer whale.

From that night on, he and his descendants claimed the crest of the killer whale and used it on their house fronts and totem poles.

* * *

The Loon Guide

Tlingit

When the world was young, a party of Tlingit were fishing in their canoes in Shrimp Bay. Suddenly it became so dark that the fishermen could neither find the shore nor the way out of the bay to their distant village. Then they heard the strange, wild cry of a loon not far from their canoes. They paddled swiftly in the direction of the sound. Soon they saw a big loon swimming slowly, just ahead of their canoes. They decided to follow the bird.

Sometimes they could not even see the white markings on the bird, in the darkness, but they could always hear its whistling cries. They followed the swift-swimming bird for a long time. At last they came out of darkness into sunlight, clear of the bay in which they had been imprisoned.

From then on, the loon has been the special crest of these Tlingit and their descendants.

* * *

The Fireweed Talking Stick

Tsimshian

The nephew of a Tsimshian chief fasted. He fasted for many suns, because it was winter; snow lay as deep as a man was tall, and he was going to hunt. All his skill as a hunter would be needed, to find animals so that he might take food and furs back to his village. He took traps and snares with him, for he hoped to trap mink, marten, rabbits, and other small animals, if he could find any.

The young man traveled far, until he saw tracks and signs of animals; then he set snares and built deadfalls along a narrow trail which followed a stream and the edge of the forest. One night, while he slept in his snow shelter, he was awakened by a bright light. He went out into the clearing, beside his shelter, and saw a great fireweed which glowed with crimson fire. The great single stalk, with its bright red flower, reached high into the sky.

The young man knew that he had had a vision. Since the sun would come soon, he set out along his line of traps. Before he had gone far, he looked back at the great fireweed. It had disappeared.

Good fortune favored his hunting that day and he also found animals in his traps. When he returned to his distant village, he told his uncle about his vision. They held a council of their clan, at which it was decided to use the fireweed from that time on, as the clan crest. The single fireweed may be seen today on the talking stick of their descendants.

* * *

Two Tests—Three Totems

Tsimshian

A poor little orphan boy grew up in a Tsimshian village. Though the tribal chief of the village was his mother's brother, the little boy was treated very badly, because he was not strong and had skin trouble. The other boys made fun of him and would not let him join in their games.

Only his old grandmother, who was too poor to help him, took notice of him. "Pray often and purify yourself," she told him, "and then you will be strong and play with the other boys."

He followed the advice of his grandmother, prayed often to the Sky Chief, took many baths in the ocean and icy streams to cleanse himself, and ran often in the forest and along the sandy beach. He twisted the branches of trees and bushes to strengthen his hands, arms, and shoulders, and swam in the ocean and lakes. He became a little stronger and cleaner with each new snow but still his skin trouble was not cured. Even when he became a young man nobody seemed to notice him. He was very sad but his grandmother told him to keep on praying and believing, and the Sky Chief would surely take pity on him and help him.

One night the poor young man's uncle, who was still the chief of the village, went down to the beach. He looked up into the sky and saw flashes of fire which lit up the village. One bright flash came straight down like a small sheet of fire. It hung from the end of a branch which stuck out from the top of a great cedar directly behind his house. When the sun came, the chief saw where the flame had hung on the branch, but in the darkness it had changed into a big copper shield. He knew that it was worth many sea-otter skins and tried to reach it by climbing high into the tree, but he could not get near it. He then tried to knock it from the branch by throwing stones and clubs, which he carried up into the cedar, but he could not hit the copper, nor could he throw high enough from the ground to reach it. The chief asked his councilors for advice. They were afraid that the copper would be spoiled if they tried to shoot it down, even with blunt-ended arrows. They advised the chief to ask the young men of the village to try and knock it down with round stones, when daylight came next day.

The chief called his people together and said, "A copper hangs from a branch of the great tree beside my house. Tomorrow, when the sun comes, the young men will try to knock it from the branch with round stones. I will give my daughter, the princess, to the young man who brings down the copper for me."

That night, the poor young man went down to the beach. A tall stranger came up to him from the direction of the ocean and asked, "What are the tidings from your village?"

The young man told him of the mysterious copper and the chief's promise to the young men of the village.

"You must try to knock the copper down," the stranger said.

"It is very high up and I do not believe that I can throw a stone high enough and strongly enough to strike the copper from the branch," replied the poor young man.

"Believe, and you will do it," the stranger answered. He picked up four big, round pebbles from the beach and gave them to the young man. "When the sun comes, you will see that one of these stones is white, one black, one blue and one red. Throw them in that order but do not show these stones to anyone." The stranger walked toward the ocean and disappeared.

Next morning, all of the people of the village gathered in front of the huge cedar. The young men threw many stones at the copper. They threw until they were tired but none of them hit it. When the poor young man wanted to throw his stones, the other young men pushed him back until at last an old wise man commanded, "Let him try!"

The poor young man threw the white stone with such good aim that it just missed the copper and whizzed on out of sight. His next two stones also passed very close to the copper. Then he took the last stone, the red one, swung it and flung it. The stone struck the copper with a loud *clang*. It fell to the ground.

Before the poor young man could reach the copper, the other young men seized it and took it into the house of the chief. Each one said, "O chief, it was I who knocked the copper from the tree."

The chief replied, "Many of you speak with a forked tongue; you must wait until I decide which one did it."

The poor young man, who had followed the others to the house of the chief, said nothing.

When night was leaving to let morning come, a great bear growled in the village. A hunter who tried to shoot it and could not said that the bear was huge and white. Next day the chief told the people of the village that he could not decide which young man had knocked the copper down, but that he would surely give the princess to the young man who killed the white bear.

That night, when the stars rode in the sky, the poor young man walked on the beach. Again the stranger silently appeared and asked, "What are the tidings from your village?"

The young man told him of the white bear and said that soon the chief would give fine bows and arrows to the young men who dared to hunt the bear.

"Go to the house of the chief and ask for a bow and one arrow. You shall kill the bear," declared the stranger. He stepped into the mist and vanished.

The poor young man went to the house of the chief. The chief was giving each young hunter who stepped up to the fire a strong bow and two arrows. When the poor young man begged his uncle for a bow and one arrow, the other young men laughed at him. The chief would not have given him the weapon had not the old wise man advised him to do so. The old wise man smiled at the poor young man when he was given the bow and arrow but said nothing.

The hunters went out and waited for the bear to come. Just as the sun came, they saw the giant bear behind the village. They all ran toward it but the poor young man, who had become so strong from exercise that he easily passed the others, was the first to get within bowshot of the big while beast. He fired, and his arrow went through the bear's heart and quivered in a tree behind the animal. He took the arrow from the tree. It was twisted and covered with fat.

While he was getting his arrow, the other young men dipped their arrows in the blood of the dead beast and dragged it to the house of the chief. One hunter gave his arrow to the chief and said, "I killed the bear. See, the blood still falls from my arrow."

Another young man, then another, declared that he had slain the bear. Each of them wished to marry the princess and so they spoke falsely.

The chief was angry with the young men because he knew that some of them lied. "Give me all of your arrows," he commanded. "I will examine them and decide who killed the bear."

The chief looked well at the arrows. He saw that all were straight. Then, as he looked up, he saw the poor young man standing behind the others. "Is your arrow among these?" he asked.

"No, chief," replied the young man, who did not dare to call the chief "uncle."

The chief took the arrow from his nephew and examined the twisted, fat-covered shaft. Then he knew who had really killed the bear.

The wise old man, who had told the chief to give the poor young man a bow and arrow, spoke with the chief. He told him that it was the killer of the bear who had also knocked down the copper.

The chief looked at the ground and did not speak. He was ashamed because the poor young man had beaten all of the nobles and other young men of the village.

The young men were ashamed too, not because they had cheated and lied but because they had been beaten by a poor young man without warrior training.

The chief sent the people to their houses. Then, because his heart was wicked, he decided to leave the village and take all of his people with him, except the poor young man and his grandmother. He sent his clan chiefs and slaves to tell all of the families to be ready to leave in their canoes when the sun came.

Next morning the people of the village paddled silently away, because the commands of the tribal chief were always obeyed. Three people were left behind: the princess, the poor young man, and his old grandmother.

The chief had left no food in the village but the grandmother had a few strips of dried, smoked salmon. The princess would not eat it, and the young man refused to eat it so that his grandmother might

have it. Because the young man was poor and because his skin trouble
had not been completely washed away, the princess would not speak
to him. She stayed in the great house of her father that night while the
young man sat beside a fire outside of his grandmother's poor little
house. All through the night he prayed to the Sky Chief for help. As
night was leaving to let morning come he had a strange dream. Then
he knew what to do!

He ran along a narrow forest trail which bordered the river. He
went far upstream until he came out into a clearing on the shore of a
great lake surrounded by cedars. It was the lake and clearing that he
had seen in his dream. At the edge of the water he stood and shouted.
Soon the water became troubled. Big waves rolled up onto the shore
where he stood. Out of the waves came a giant frog. It was much
bigger than the young man. Its eyes were of copper and it had long,
sharp copper claws. Before it could seize him, the young man ran
swiftly back down the trail. The frog chased him but could not catch
him, so it returned to the lake.

The young man ran back to the village. When he reached the
deserted houses, he searched among them until he found a stone axe-
head. He made a strong handle for it, sharpened the head, and returned to the clearing beside the lake. He chopped down a cedar so
that it fell across the trail. One end of the tree rested on top of a rock
beside the trail. Then he levered one end of the log up and set it on a
trigger made from a straight sapling. He drove a wedge to hold the
deadfall trap log in place. He climbed under the deadfall and found
that he had to wriggle to get through onto the trail.

The young man went to the shore of the lake. He prayed to the
Sky Chief, then shouted loudly four times. Almost at once the huge
frog came to the surface and swam swiftly toward the shore. The
young man, pursued by the frog, raced quickly toward the deadfall
and wriggled under the big log. The frog tried to follow him but it
could not squeeze under. Before it could back out from under the
heavy log, the young man seized the heavy axe and knocked out the
wedge which held the trap in place. It crashed down on the frog and
killed it.

The young man drove wedges between the rock and the log so
that he could pull the giant frog clear. Slowly and with great difficulty
he eased the beast from under the deadfall. He skinned the frog,
leaving the claws on, and slipped into the skin. It was a little too big
but the arms and legs fitted very well. He kept the skin on by lacing it
up the front with a strong, thin cedar root.

Soon the young man felt quite comfortable inside the frog skin.

He dived into the lake and hopped along the bottom. With the copper claws, he caught a fine big trout and swam with it to the edge of the lake. He went ashore, took off the frog skin and hid it safely in a hollow tree before returning, as darkness came, to the village. He placed the trout on the beach in front of the chief's house.

In the morning, a raven cawed loudly on the beach. It awakened the princess. She went to the door and called to the poor young man. She called as though she spoke to a slave. When the young man came, she told him to see why the raven called. He went down to the beach and returned with the trout. "The raven found it," he told the princess.

He offered to cook the fish for her but she refused, so the young man gave the trout to his grandmother. The old woman was glad to get it. She was very hungry. She ate all of it when her grandson told her that he was not hungry. He *was* hungry, but he fasted to gain more power.

That night, wearing the frog skin, the young man caught a much bigger trout and put it on the beach as before. Once again the raven cawed and the princess called. The young man went and got the fish. He was very glad when the princess noticed him and spoke with him for a short while because though she was proud, as the daughter of a chief and noble had the right to be, she was very beautiful and the young man was greatly in love with her. The princess was beginning to notice the young man because his skin trouble was almost gone and he looked clean and straight and strong.

That night the young man again prayed to the Sky Chief for help before putting on the frog skin on the shore of the lake. Afterward, he swam and walked along the bottom of the lake into the river, which ran from the lake into the ocean. He swam down the river into the ocean. Here he caught a huge salmon and dragged it up onto the sand in front of the chief's house. This time when the raven called, the princess went to see why. The young man ran to her and she gladly ate some of the salmon. The young man was glad.

When darkness came, the princess hid behind a great cedar and saw the young man rise from the fire and run into the forest. She followed behind him and kept watch beside the ocean until the sun came. Then she was astonished to see a great frog carrying a big salmon come out of the ocean and walk onto the beach. She was even more astonished when she saw the young man step out of the frog skin. He pulled the salmon up in front of her house and disappeared into the forest.

A little later, when the raven called, the princess ran to the beach and met the young man beside the salmon. He was now clean and radiant and the daughter of the chief knew that she loved him.

"I know that it was you who caught the trout and the salmon. The raven did not find them. You are a good fisherman," the princess told him.

"It is true, princess," he replied, "and now that you have noticed me I am glad and proud and will become a good hunter and warrior too."

They had just finished feasting on the salmon when the young man saw the mysterious stranger who had advised him to throw at the copper and shoot at the bear. He walked toward them from the ocean but they saw no canoe. He was wearing the rich ceremonial robes and high, cone-shaped hat of a shaman and chief.

"The winds told me that one who has the right to make two one should be here at this time," he said with a serene smile.

He married them and the poor young man lived happily with his princess. He became a chief among his people when they returned to the distant village, after their cruel chief had been killed by a white bear.

The young chief rightly took for his totems a copper, a bear and a frog. His totem pole, which was set up with great ceremony, potlatching and feasting, showed at its base a great white bear holding a copper between its paws. The top of the great red cedar pole was carved and painted to represent a huge frog with long, sharp claws. The new chief's grandmother lived, proudly and happily, in a fine new cedar house which he built for her.

✳ ✳ ✳

Master Carver

Haida

When the world was young, the Haida did not know the art of carving. Then a strange being came to them. He was surrounded by a bright light. He wore a shirt made from the wool of mountain goats and covered with strange designs. His headdress was carved from wood and painted in different colors. His body was covered with

tattooed crests and designs. What the Haida found most astonishing, after marveling at the bright light, was his fingernails. On each nail was a human face and each face was different, as was its expression and design. When this man, whom they later learned to call Master Carver, arrived at the chief Haida village, he told the people, "Something strange will happen tonight. Do not think about it. When darkness comes, sleep. Above all things, do not look out of your houses or come from them until you see that the sun has risen."

The Haida sensed that the stranger had much spirit power, so they obeyed him. That night, the people heard the sounds of chopping and the fall of trees, but they stayed under their blankets, as they had been told to do. The sun was high before they left their houses. Then they saw that the corner posts of the great community house had been carved, and the cedar partition at the back end of the house was painted with the figures of humans and animals. When they went out into the sunlight, they were astonished to see three carved poles, painted and fixed to the front of the house. There was a pole directly in the middle and another at each corner of the housefront. All of the housefront was covered with carvings and paintings. Strange figures of humans, animals, birds, and fish stared at the Haida from the front of the house. The people were amazed and frightened because never before had they seen such things.

Master Carver told the people to look well at everything he had done and then try to copy them. They thought about it and looked hard at the wonderful work. Some of the men copied it very well.

Master Carver was pleased with their efforts and returned, from time to time, to teach them more of his art. Every day he showed the best workers one of the paintings on his fingernails, told them what it meant, and taught them to copy it.

So it was that the Haida learned the art of carving and painting, and the secrets to be told on the talking sticks which they learned to make. Today, a splendid totem pole may still be seen which tells of Master Carver and his work.

* * *

The First Totem Pole

Northwest Coast

Young Otter walked sadly along the bank of a clear flowing river. It was summer, the sun shone and the young man should have been glad but there was little brightness in the warrior's heart. He was sad because the fame once foretold by a powerful medicine man had not yet touched him. Many, many seasons ago the shaman had told the young man's mother that her son would become famous among the Indians of the Northwest Coast while he was still young. He would perform a feat, the medicine man said, that would make him remembered by the Northwest tribes long after the wartime feats of greater warriors were forgotten. Between tribal wars, in which Young Otter and his two brothers had fought bravely, he always hoped for the chance that would make him noticed by his chiefs. Thus far, that chance had never come.

His path led him to the spring-that-always-bubbles. There he found his brothers sitting on the bank of the steaming pool which surrounded the hot spring. He stooped to look into the depths of the quivering water and jumped back with a shout of surprise and fear, for he saw a giant figure slowly and silently rise from the center of the bubbling spring. Slowly, slowly, higher and higher, the man-like form rose until it towered high above Young Otter's head. He saw that the figure looked like a seated man hewn from a block of stone. The figure's hands hung at his sides. What surprised Young Otter most was that seven young ravens were perched like a headdress on the figure's head.

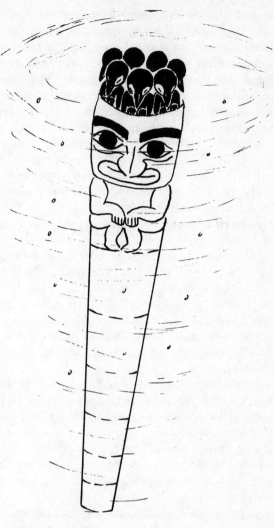

Young Otter's two brothers leapt to their feet and stood as though frozen, but Young Otter ran swiftly toward the village to ask the chiefs and wise men to come and see the magic figure, in case it should suddenly decide to disappear into the heart of the deep spring from which it had come. When Young Otter was able to make the chiefs and villagers believe that what he had just seen was not a dream, they ran after him to the pool. What they saw startled and frightened them. Not even the chiefs dared go close to the magic figure. Strangely enough, fear had gone from Young Otter. He went as close to the figure as he could and begged his friends to help him drag it from the spring. They were afraid but at last, by giving gifts and promising still more, he got some of the younger men and older warriors to help him to pull the figure from the spring onto the bank. When the people saw that the figure did not move and made no magic to harm them, they helped Young Otter to move it on log rollers up the hill toward Young Otter's house. Soon more and more people pushed and pulled, girls sang pull-away songs, until at last the figure stood just in front of Young Otter's house which looked out on the beach and ocean. "See, mother," Young Otter whispered as she stood astonished in the doorway of the cedar plank house, "this may be the beginning of the good fortune that the medicine man told you of."

Tired and worn out by their hard work, Young Otter and his helpers slept soundly until the sun was high in the sky the next day. Then once again, they gathered in wonder around the great figure which still lay where they had left it. "We must make this magic man stand up," said Young Otter. "It is not good that he lies on the ground."

The older men said that a hole would have to be dug in the ground for the man to stand up in. "The hole must be deep and it will take many people and strong ropes of cedar fiber to set him upright in it," said a clan chief.

"I am sure that the man will stand up if we set him on end," exclaimed Young Otter. He wondered afterward why he had thought so. It seemed most likely that the great figure would fall over if they set it on end without any support.

Since Young Otter promised to hold a potlatch and give away many blankets and other presents at the feast, which would follow the setting up of the pole-of-the-magic-figure, willing helpers ran off to get long push-poles and pull-ropes to do the work.

After a long time and much hard work, the tall pole-like figure at last stood firmly on end directly in front of Young Otter's house. To everyone's great surprise, it did not fall over. Pushing it did not even shake it. A chief pointed out that the figure did not even lean toward the sea, though it stood at the top of the slope facing the beach.

Joyfully, Young Otter sent messengers to the neighboring tribes telling them of the great magic man and inviting them to come to his potlatch on the night when the moon was round, which was only four suns away.

At daylight, ready to go fishing in preparation for his feast, Young

Otter stood with his two brothers at the door of his house. All three stared in never-dying wonder at the huge figure before them. Then Young Otter gave a loud shout, because the magic man suddenly moved. Surely, slowly the figure started to move toward the ocean.

In an instant, forgetting their fears in their desire to keep the figure where it was, Young Otter and his brothers tried to hold the great form back. Their efforts were useless and even with the help of many of their people, who lost their fear in their excitement, they could not stop the slow, downhill movement of the magic man toward the ocean.

Slowly, surely, serenely, the figure reached the beach. Young Otter hoped that it would have to stop on the soft sand there, but it did not. Pushing aside big dugout canoes as though they were twigs, the figure moved across the wide beach into the ocean. Soon it was up to its knees in water, then its waist and shoulders sank from sight. Only its raven-crowned head remained for a moment above water— then it was gone.

The chiefs and people were sad and angry. They blamed Young Otter for not having had his helpers stand the magic man in a deep hole. "He would still be with us if you had done that thing," an angry chief told Young Otter. "When our visitors arrive and we have no magic man to show them we shall be shamed forever."

What caused the proud people most sorrow was that when the neighboring tribes would come to see the wonder, it would be gone. Then the visitors would mock and declare that it had never been. They might even make war for having been so greatly deceived.

That night Young Otter hid deep in the forest and prayed hard until the sun came. Then he went back to the village, for he knew what to do. He got tools and helpers, who still hoped that there would be a potlatch, and returned to the forest. There they cut down a great cedar, using fire and axe to make it fall, as they did when they cut great cedars to make canoes. As soon as the forest giant lay on the ground, Young Otter started to carve a figure on its trunk. His helpers cut away the rest of the tree, leaving only a long pole.

Until the sun left to let darkness come, Young Otter cut and carved. All next day, he worked again. The chiefs and people of the village were astonished to see how much like the lost magic man the figure became as Young Otter worked. The young man did not tire and his hands seemed to be guided. Even the ravens on the figure's head began to look like real ravens as the moon rose on the second day. Throughout the next morning, Young Otter worked and the sun was directly overhead when the figure was finished. Even the chiefs and wise men could find no difference between the figure and the magic man who had disappeared.

Gladly, all of the people rolled and pulled the great carved cedar pole into place before Young Otter's house. Then a great hole was dug, one side of it sloping downward, so that the foot of the pole could be slid into it. Some of the people pulled on ropes tied to the pole, while some pushed. Others piled stones and put earth around the foot of the great carved pole as it at last stood upright. Nobody could tell that it was not the same figure that had stood there three suns ago.

When the tribes came to Young Otter's potlatch, they were afraid and astonished when they looked up at the huge raven-crowned figure. Never had they seen or heard of anything like it. They thought that it was powerful magic and praised Young Otter for his fearlessness in being the first to touch it and having no fear of it. Young Otter became famous and was honored by his tribe.

To this day, the Indians of the Northwest Coast cut and carve figures on great cedar poles. They have long tried to copy the magic and wonder of The First Totem Pole.

* * *

Talking Stick Vision
Haida

So long ago that the time cannot be counted by suns or moons, a Haida chief and his son, who was a prince, set out from the islands of their people in a great canoe for the mainland. They went to get much food and oil for a big feast. When the trading was over, they started the homeward voyage. As they passed one of the many islands, not far from the village where they lived, the prince had a vision. He looked over the side of the canoe and saw a village of fine houses on the ocean floor. Great poles, the like of which he had never seen, stood in front of some of the houses. One splendid pole, taller than the rest, stood in front of a great house, maybe the house of the chief. The prince could clearly see the figures and carvings on the pole, but they were of a sort unknown to him.

When the vision faded and the prince could speak, he told his father about the village beneath the ocean, off the Rosespit, at the

northeast point of the islands of the Haida, and of the wonderful pole which stood in front of the dwelling of the underseas chief.

The chief knew that his son had had a vision. He decided to call some of the Haida carvers who did the best work, and make a copy of the pole which the prince had seen and remembered so well. The carvers worked hard and a great feast was proclaimed for the day when the pole would be ready to set in place in the ground. Invitations were sent to chiefs and royal families on the islands and on the mainland. Many promised to attend the feast.

On the day then the pole was finished, many great canoes were on the ocean close to the village of Skidegate, on the way to the feast. A high tide, far higher than any that had been seen in the ocean surrounding the islands until that time, picked up the canoes and carried them high up onto the beach of the island where the feastgiver lived.

The people of the village and the visitors were greatly surprised but they got ready to pull the great pole into place. They were hauling on ropes and the foot of the pole lay close to the deep hole which had been dug to receive it when another great tide swept up on the beach. It covered all of the island. The guests were changed by some powerful magic into great black and white puffins with red bills. They flew away and disappeared over the ocean. The great pole came to life and swam far out into the ocean where it was lost to view.

The people of the island were very angry and blamed the prince and his father for the trouble which had come upon them. They believed that what had happened was because the pole which the prince had seen on the ocean floor was taboo. It was much too sacred to be copied, they thought, and that is why misfortune came to them.

* * *

The Magic Totem Pole
Northwest Coast

Northwest coast tribes tell this story. The people wondered and were angry. Their young chief, Yahkdsi, was becoming more and more lazy. He became selfish and neglected his duties as tribal chief. Had he been old, they would have understood, but Yahkdsi was young, strong and active in his own interests, while he forgot the needs of his people.

Counselors and wise men met and decided that since their chief would not change his idle ways, they would end his rule. The young chief was not bad or cruel, so they did not kill him. They had other plans. One night, when Yahkdsi returned from a day spent resting in the forest, he found that his tribe had gone and the village had been destroyed by fire. The young chief felt very sorry for himself. He knew that the neighboring tribes were unfriendly. He dared not seek shelter in their territory. The canoes were gone and so was all of the winter food supply. Signs told him that the destruction of the village and departure of the people had not been caused by enemy raiders. His people had left him of their own accord.

Yahkdsi mourned over the ashes of his once fine house. "My people were cruel to desert me," he cried aloud. Then he looked into his heart and found the reason why. "I am to blame! It is all my fault!" he said.

As he spoke these words, a being that smelt of the ocean stood suddenly beside him. The figure was huge, seaweed-decked, shadowy, and strange. The young chief was afraid. He knew that what stood over him was a supernatural sea spirit from the mysterious spirit world of the ocean. Yahkdsi tried to cover his eyes with his hands but they were frozen to his sides with fear.

"I know that now you are sorry for your neglect of your people," said the sea spirit. "Now you know that a chief must think first of his people and then of himself. You shall have another chance, because your heart tells you that you were wrong."

Even as the sea spirit spoke, the young chief found himself crouching outside a fine house. A good-looking young woman stood beside the little oval doorway in the fine frontal pole of the dwelling.

"She is your spirit wife," the sea spirit told the young chief. "Be good to her at all times, or she will leave you and your good fortune will go with her."

Before Yahkdsi could thank the spirit thing, it glided down the beach and disappeared with the soft noise of waves breaking on a sandy shore. Then the young chief saw that a splendid totem pole towered between the house and the ocean. His wife came to him and together they looked at the finely carved and painted pole. A great eagle with folded wings perched on top of the pole, and at the foot an octopus, with its eight tentacles spread out in front of it, looked out toward the ocean.

Yahkdsi sprang swiftly back. "I saw the sea thing move," he shouted to his wife.

"Maybe so," she replied calmly. "It is a magic totem pole."

With a wife to help and encourage him, the young chief became a man. He hunted and fished and worked as he had never done before and made his wife, Sea Song, glad.

Early one morning, the chief heard the loud scream of an eagle outside the house. He put his head through the doorway and looked out. What he saw so amazed him that he shouted.

The eagle that screamed was the one on top of the totem pole. It flapped its strong wings and a loud, sharp *Kre-e-e-e* came from its open beak. The octopus stretched out its long tentacles oceanward and seized a seal which was being washed onto the beach. While Yahkdsi stared in amazement, the octopus dragged the seal up the beach and flung it alongside the house.

The chief ran to the totem pole and gazed at the eagle and octopus with startled eyes. They were both quite still again and the great eagle sat with folded wings. The chief turned to Sea Song who had followed him from the house.

"I told you that it was a magic totem pole, my husband," she said, and laughter lurked in her sea-green eyes.

From then on, the eagle screamed to tell of food that was washed onto the beach and the tentacles of the octopus whipped the ocean-borne food up to the house before the sea creatures could escape back into deep water.

One sun-filled morning, the young chief saw canoes riding on the calm ocean in front of his house. His tribe, which had learned of their former chief's good fortune, had returned in the hope of sharing it with him. Things had gone badly with the people since they had burned and left their village. They were in great need. Yahkdsi was not friendly to the wise men who came ashore to ask that the people might return.

"Many moons have passed since you deserted me," he told them angrily, "and now you seek my pity and help."

"Forgive your people," Sea Song begged. "Only great chiefs are great enough to forgive."

The young chief followed his wife's counsel and forgave his tribe. The canoes were beached and soon a newer and better village than before stood facing the ocean.

The people asked Yahkdsi to be their chief again and, after speaking with Sea Song, he agreed.

This time, he ruled as a good chief should and his people were glad and prospered. Soon Yahkdsi became more and more occupied with potlatches and more and more preoccupied with material things. Sea Song was neglected and became more and more shadowy with each passing sun.

The young chief noticed this too late. One night, as he spoke with her before the fire in their great house, her voice became fainter and fainter. While he watched her, she became more like a spirit shadow than a woman. Then she was gone, and Yahkdsi felt the winds of winter blow sharply on him. He looked around. The house was gone. In the cold white moonlight, he saw that the magic totem pole was no longer in front of where the house had been; it too had disappeared.

Only a memorial totem pole, commemorating the young chief, can be seen today. The magic is gone. No longer does the eagle scream or the octopus stretch out its tentacles.

✳   ✳   ✳

The Weeping Totem Pole
Haida

He-Who-Never-Frowns was Chief of the Northern Island. The Haida people were happy because he was very wise and lived at peace with

the other tribes of the surrounding islands. The old chief felt that the
Great Spirit was good to his children so long as they lived peacefully
and never killed birds, animals, or fish unless they were needed for
food and clothing.

When this chief was told by one of his scouts that there were fine,
fat deer on an island called Tanu, he ordered a big hunting party to
get ready. Before the sun was high, seven big canoes filled with hunters left the northern island for Tanu. The chief's many sons and two
young grandsons went with them. The canoes reached Tanu as the sun

sank. Soon a fire, started with rubbing sticks, blazed at the edge of the forest.

When the sun came again, the hunters left in little hunting parties to look for the deer. The chief left his two grandsons in camp. "Guard well the fire," he told them. "It is easier to keep a fire alight than to light one."

"We will keep the fire burning brightly," the boys promised.

That night, when the chief and hunters returned to camp, the fire was dead. Charred logs and branches lay all around. Not even a live spark could be found. The two boys were nowhere to be seen. Warriors found them hiding in the bushes.

"Why did you let the fire go out?" the chief asked them sternly.

"The frogs put it out," the older boy told him in a voice that trembled.

"Yes," agreed the other grandson. "When we were getting wood, we found a big frog. We threw it into the fire. It swelled up and burst with much noise, so we threw other frogs on the fire. They too made a big noise when they burst."

"It was the last frog that put the fire out," the bigger boy explained. "It made a noise like thunder. Logs and sticks were thrown from the fire and it died quicker than a gull dives."

"We are lost," cried the chief. "We are lost because of your badness! You both know well that the Great Spirit punishes those who hurt his creatures needlessly. Run to the canoes. Leave the deer here," he commanded.

The hunters started to run to the canoes. Thunder roared and lightning flashed. The earth shook. Great trees crashed to the ground. Fire spouted from the earth. A great hole opened in the earth and swallowed all of the hunters. Only the old chief was spared by the Great Spirit.

When He-Who-Never-Frowns reached the northern island, he was so changed and sad that his people called him "He-Who-Weeps-For-His-Children." Soon he died of grief and his relatives set up a great cedar totem pole in his honor. On it was carved a figure of He-Who-Weeps-For-His-Children, holding a frog in his hands. A great stream of tears fell from each eye of the old chief onto the head of a grandson. Below the figures of the two boys, was the face of a huge frog.

The pole was known as the totem pole of the Chief-Who-Weeps. It may still be seen.

✳ ✳ ✳

The First Potlatch

Northwest Coast

When the world was young, a great bird with many-colored feathers landed on the ocean in front of an Indian village of the Northwest coast. The young men of the tribe tried to shoot it. They hunted it from the beach and from their canoes. None was successful.

A chief named Golden Eagle stood on the beach with his slave, Blue Jay. The chief saw with sorrow what poor hunters his young men were. "Even my young children could kill that strange bird!" he exclaimed.

"But they are girls!" cried the surprised slave, who knew that girls were not supposed to hunt birds and game.

The chief did not answer. His two daughters had been standing inside a house on the beach, not far off. They had heard the words of their father. Without saying that they had heard, they spent the next few days secretly in the forest, finding arrow-wood for arrows and making a strong yew bow. They hid the bow and arrows in a great, hollow cedar tree.

One morning before the sun came, they slipped into the forest. There they put on boys' clothes and combed their long hair in front of their faces so that they would not look like the daughters of a chief. Then they took the hidden bow and arrows and went down to the beach. They found only a small fishing canoe there.

All of the young men were out in the other canoes, hunting for the "magic rainbow bird." When the girls had paddled a little distance from shore, they saw the bird fly up from out of a circle of canoes which had surrounded it. The younger girl paddled silently until they came within bowshot of the bird which had landed on the ocean again. The older girl, who had practiced often with a bow in the forest, fired only one arrow. It entered the bird's heart. Swiftly pulling the big bird from the ocean, the two girls paddled quickly to land before the surprised warriors, in their big canoes, could head them off.

The girls hid the beautiful bird deep in the forest and then told their father what they had done. The chief scolded them for having hunted the bird, but in his heart he was glad because of his daughters' skill.

"We wanted the bird so that we might give its rainbow feathers to our bird friends," explained the older daughter.

This spirit of giving pleased the chief. He decided to give a big feast the next night, so that his daughters could give away the feathers when the feasting was finished.

Next morning, just as the sun came, Blue Jay started to give out many gift sticks, which were invitations to the feast, and all day long the big invitation drum sounded from in front of Golden Eagle's house.

Just as the sun was leaving, a great flock of many kinds of birds gathered at the house of Golden Eagle. After a great feast, Golden Eagle proudly told of his daughters' skill as hunters and said that they now wished to give presents to all of their guests. Then the daughters brought in the bird, which seemed to glow with many-colored fires, and began their feather gift-giving ceremony. To the wood duck they gave lovely feathers of gray, green, red, blue, white, and buff. The meadow lark was given feathers of brown and yellow. Light blue, dark blue, and white feathers were given to the kingfisher. The western tanager was made gay with feathers of red, yellow, and black. Many more birds were given feathers before the ceremony ended.

Since that give-away feast, which they called a potlatch, the birds have worn the colorful feathers given them and there have been many, many more potlatches.

*　　*　　*

The Potlatch of Tight Fist
Northwest Coast

Tight Fist and his wife sat in front of their fine cedar-plank house in the Nootka village. Though the late afternoon sun shone brightly upon them, neither was glad. The dark shadows of unhappiness which lay on their hearts could not be chased away, because the wife of Tight Fist had many sad thoughts in her mind, and her husband did not know why dark thoughts were inside his mind. "Why should I not be glad," he thought. "We are well and strong for our ages, and we do not want for anything. Dried salmon and halibut hang heavy on our racks; we have much eulachon oil and many dried berries in our food boxes; we have many fine blankets and skins; so why should my wife hang her head? Perhaps," he thought, "that is what makes me walk in the dark shadows." But he knew that this was not so.

On the sandy beach of the village, a group of young people were talking quietly together. "That is what we should do," declared a young man earnestly.

"You speak well and truly," said a young woman of the clan.

"Tight Fist has so much, and so many of our people have so little. Although Tight Fist has many blankets, and salmon, oil, and food stored away in his food chests, he has never once sent out invitations to a potlatch. All of our chiefs, even those with few things of value, have given at least one potlatch give-away feast because they like to give," said another villager.

"That is why they are chiefs," said a tall young fisherman, who was carrying a whale lance.

"And maybe that is why Tight Fist is not," added a young man who was wearing a dance apron.

They talked much and earnestly until the dark blanket of night was covering the ocean. Then, just as they were about to go to their homes, one of the older of the young people in the group had a wonderful idea. "Let us force old Tight Fist to give a potlatch!"

The rest of the group were too astonished to reply for some time. They knew that nobody had ever been made to give a potlatch; never, in all of the years of their lives that they could remember, had such a big thing happened. They knew that such a thing could be made to happen, but always the person giving the potlatch did so because he wanted to. All of the villagers on that part of the seacoast had wanted to give such a feast, just as soon as they had enough gifts and food to make it possible. Other people giving these feasts sometimes worked hard for years to get enough good things together to be as liberal as they wanted to be. But Tight Fist was different from these people.

There was much to be done, and the most difficult thing of all was to keep the idea a complete secret from the ears of Tight Fist and his wife. The young planners knew that all of the others in the village would say nothing until the surprise was sprung, like a clever trap. The heralds were told first, because it was their duty to announce all such feasts, when they were told to do so. They were astonished when they were told that the potlatch was being given by Tight Fist, and that the feast was to be announced loudly in all parts of the village only a half hour before the drums announced the commencement of the feast. The secret planners did not tell the heralds that every family in the village was being told, with many chuckles, where, when, and by whom the potlatch was being given.

The sun had gone to let the moon come when the villagers heard the voices of the heralds announcing the festival. Only Tight Fist and his wife did not hear what the heralds cried, since it had been planned that no heralds would cry out the news near the house of Tight Fist; and their voices, in other parts of the village, were not heard by the victims of the prank because they had the doors tightly closed, as they sat in front of a small fire. They sat close to the flame because the master of the house did not believe in wasting much wood when only a little would still give heat.

Only when drums began beating all over the village did Tight Fist learn that something very big was taking place or had already happened. While he and his wife were wondering what could have happened, they heard the roll of the drums and the drumming on beating-boards coming closer and closer to his house. Then they saw the flame of many bright-burning torches just outside. When Tight Fist had recovered from his surprise enough to look out through his house-post doorway, he saw a crowd of villagers gathered and still gathering in a big square in front of his house. Then he learned from the loud voiceof a herald nearby that he, Tight Fist, was inviting all of the villagers to his potlatch.

He climbed through the doorway in a daze, but still he greeted the villagers cheerfully, welcoming them all to his potlatch. "Tight Fist is stingy but he is not unwise, and maybe the Great Spirit has spoken to his heart," the people thought.

The wife of he-who-gave-little came shyly through the small doorway, but her face shone in the torchlight with a proud smile as she added her welcome to that of her husband. The music sounded loud as the villagers danced happily in the big square which they formed in front of the house. To her amazement, the wife of Tight Fist was asked to dance, first by her husband, who danced very well, although she had never known him to dance before. Then one of the chiefs asked her to dance and treated her like a princess.

Then, to the wonder of all, Tight Fist demanded a challenge dance in which he would try to outdance three of the young men dancers. Though all of the villagers felt sure that the challenge must be some form of joke, they were so happy that Tight Fist was showing such courtesy and good humor in such difficult circumstances, that they did announce that three of the very best dancers among the young men would try their dancing skill against that of the generous giver of the potlatch.

Tight Fist put on a splendid dance apron and advanced to the center of the square to meet the three smiling young men. Then they danced! And how they danced! The young men, polite as all of the villagers were at such ceremonies, began with a few easy steps which they thought would not be too difficult for the old man to follow. They were not, as the "old" man danced higher and twirled quicker than the young dancers. Not only the young men saw that they were meeting a real challenge, but the drummers sensed it too. As the villagers looked on in wonder, the drums beat out a very fast rhythm, and the legs and bodies of the dancers leapt and turned and twisted to meet the challenge. The skillful drummers added to the difficulty of the many steps by making sudden changes in tempo, at the most unexpected moment, but still the dance continued without a flaw. When it was seen that Tight Fist could not be defeated, a chief announced that the older man was the winner, and the young dancers left the square with their arms over Tight Fist's shoulders.

The dancing and singing continued for a long time; then the wife of Tight Fist, her face beaming, beckoned to her husband, who was surrounded by villagers. Then he went to the doorway of his house and invited all to follow him in to the feast which the women had prepared. The chiefs led the way and when all had passed through the doorway into the great house, there was much feasting. There was plenty of everything on which to feast, and everything was of the best.

When the sun was high, and the last of the feasters had left, Tight Fist and his wife gazed around at the empty fish racks and the empty food chests, but the old couple were still smiling happily.

Then the chief of the village and the medicine-working shaman came in through the doorway. They had come, they said, to invite Tight Fist to take part in a meeting of the village council which was going to be held on the next day.

"I am honored, O Chief and Shaman," stammered Tight Fist, "but you will all see a very poor man in council."

"You will be one among others," said the chief with a smile, "but we do not look upon the poor men, but upon their rich hearts."

✻ ✻ ✻

Medicine Men, Transformers, Tricksters, and Witches

The Loon's Necklace

Iroquois

The medicine man was sad, and for good reason, as he sat facing the bright beams of the afternoon sun. A sky of shimmering blue crowned the fragrant forest. It was the Moon of Painted Leaves. The hardwood trees were tinted with scarlet, copper, orange-red and tawny shades. The quivering leaves of the birch shone like burnished gold, reflecting the mellow, golden light of the sun and the black spires of spruce and pine towered skyward just beyond a village of the Iroquois. Overhead, a golden eagle drifted in the cloudless sky, but the eyes of the medicine man did not follow the wonder of its effortless floating. He felt the warm touch of summer on his face. His keen ears heard the faintest rustle of the woodland wild folk, but he saw them not. Dark Night, the medicine man, was sad because he was blind. As he sat in front of his lodge, he heard the voice of his scolding wife. She added to his sorrow by her constant complaints.

"Why weave you not blankets or make arrows like other men who live in the night shadows?" she grumbled. "If you did we could trade such things for food and skins. Then we would not know hunger and cold, as we will when snow flies. People now pay you little for your advice as a medicine man. They say that you only know things by fours and that four cannot be strong medicine, cannot cure their ills. All you can think of and say is 'four.' Our people laugh now when you say, 'When the owl hoots four times, seek spruce sap for your cough.' Or, 'Place four white pebbles on the red rock by the lakeshore on the fourth day,'" she mocked cruelly.

Dark Night heard, but he was patient. "Four is my medicine sign," he told her. "I learned it in my dream when my secret totem and medicine animal were revealed."

"Why not call on your totem to help us now?" demanded his wife.

"When the time comes, I will," he promised patiently.

Only when he heard the quavering laugh of a loon come from a nearby lake did the sad look leave his face. Then he would smile and listen, and his lips would move in unspoken answers to the wild calls.

The painted leaves fell. A wild wind blew from the north. Winter came.

The fear of hunger flowed like mist in the hearts of the people. A black cloud of fear hung over the lodges of the tribe. Even before the Snow Moon, hunting had been bad. With the snow it became worse. Bands of hunters returned to the village with the same story: neither animals nor birds were to be found. Lone hunters, the best in the tribe, brought back no game, even after long, cold days on the trail. Then the chief sent his young men to the neighboring tribes with beads and weapons to trade for food. They returned with the same trade goods which they had taken with them. Their friendly neighbors also sought food in vain. There was none to spare. Then, when the Hunger Moon shone in the sad sky, there was none at all.

One night of bitter cold, lying awake in his lodge, Dark Night heard four times the wild, quavering, warning cry of a loon flying directly overhead. Instantly the medicine man dozed and dreamed. In his troubled sleep his mind's eye saw a vision of sorrow, famine, danger and death. Throughout his dream he heard always the unearthly, high-pitched, savage attack cry of wolves coming ever nearer. Four loud, haunting loon laughs awoke him. Sleep suddenly left him, but the dream stayed in his mind. The awful attack call of the wolf packs and the four warning calls of the loon were still in his mind when night left to let daybreak come.

When the sun shone, he groped his way to the council lodge. Inside, the chief of the band sat in council with the tribal medicine man and the wisest men of the tribe. Dark Night stood before them. "This is how it will be," he warned them. He told of his dream and the coming attack by wolf packs in four days' time. Those in council silently mocked him.

"Were the shadows of hunger not in my heart, I would laugh," the tribal medicine man declared. The Wise Ones smiled pityingly but were silent.

When they heard of Dark Night's warning, the people of the village made fun of him. They had ceased to respect or fear his power as a medicine man. They pointed their fingers at him and tried to forget their hunger in their silent mockery.

At the end of the fourth day, as night spread its dark, star-studded blanket over the village, the mockers heard the savage cry of wolves. Fear spread like fire in the hearts of the people. They were terror-filled, silent and stunned, as fierce, starving wolf packs arrived. That night the hungry beasts raided the village. They tore men and women and carried off children before the beasts could be driven away with fire and weapons. Each night the blood-thirsty wolves attacked and for days even the bravest warriors feared to leave the village.

Then the chief sent his tribal medicine man to Dark Night and begged him to come to the council lodge. At once he obeyed his chief and followed the well-beaten trail through the deep snow to the meeting place. This time the desperate chief and his councilors did not mock Dark Night.

"Help us," pleaded the chief as he guided the blind medicine man to the place of honor beside him. "Tell us what to do. It has been whispered by the Wise Ones that you have a magic bow. Arrows fired from that bow, they tell, never miss. Let our best hunter use it, should the wolves come again tonight."

"No one but I can bend the magic bow," declared Dark Night, "but tonight I will use it if your young men bring me many hunting arrows."

"You shall have all of our best arrows," promised the chief. He gave orders that the warriors and young men take their finest arrows to the lodge of Dark Night at once. The wife of the medicine man received them. She was now proud of her blind husband whom she had mocked before the snow came.

That night the wolves attacked again. Dark Night, dressed in his best hunting dress, circled the village. He held his great magic bow and was guided by a great warrior who carried many arrows but no bow. When Dark Night heard the movement of a wolf, he quickly placed an arrow on the bow thong, pointed the shaft in the direction of the sound and pulled the bow taut. As the song of the bow thong whipped the darkness, the whistle of the feathered shaft was followed each time by the death howl of a wolf. The fierce snarls of the starving beasts shattered the silence of the night. With blazing eyes the wolves fought each other with blood-flecked jaws that they might devour the bodies of their fellows which had fallen to Dark Night's bow. Arrows fired by a tireless arm, flew from the bow until the pale fingers of morning groped among the trunks of the trees. Then the wolves fled, leaving many great, gray bodies stretched out on the crimson-stained snow. The starving people feasted ravenously on the slain beasts, and presents were piled high before the lodge of Dark Night. Often from that night until the snows left to let spring come, the bow of the medicine man twanged to serve his people. Then the grass came back, deer, other animals, and birds returned to the land and the people were happy again.

Late one sun-filled evening, Dark Night sat outside his fine new lodge which the grateful people had made for him. A smile was on his face and he seemed to be listening. Clearly, loudly, from the distant lake came the strange, soul-stirring cry of a loon. Four times did the quavering *wah-hoo-o-o-o-o* cry blend with the serene spring song of the fragrant forest. Once again Dark Night dressed himself in his finest buckskin. Around his neck he placed his most precious possession, a necklace of gleaming snow-white shells. Refusing the help of many willing hands, he groped his way from tree to tree toward the loon call and the lake. When the cry sounded directly in front of him, the medicine man held onto the slim trunk of a paper birch tree while he thrust the toe of his moccasin-clad foot forward. It touched the soft, yellow sand at the edge of the lake. The setting sun, which he could not see, was sinking in a flaming curtain of splendor on the calm water of the silver-misted lake. The startling call of the loon shattered the silence. Never before had Dark Night heard the notes so loud and clear and near. Trembling, the medicine man spoke. "O Father Loon, my totem bird, I have a wish which my heart prays may be granted."

"Speak my son, that I may know your desire," replied a deep, musical voice.

The words came from a point so close to Dark Night's feet that he was startled. He managed to murmur, "For many, many moons I have lived in darkness deeper than darkest night. I pray you, let my eyes see the wonders which I can only sense."

"Faith has made you believe. Faith will make you see, my son. You have been patient. Climb onto my back and hold tight to my wings."

Astonishment and fear, and a great hope, were strong in Dark Night's heart as he did as he was told. He grasped the loon's wings tightly and the great bird dived. Suddenly the medicine man felt the cold waters of the lake flow against his sightless eyes.

The loon came to the surface when the distant shore was reached. "Has the light come to your eyes, my son?"

"No, Father Loon, all is still dark."

"Hold tightly," warned the voice.

Once again the loon dived smoothly beneath the surface and swam to the opposite shore. When they reached it, Dark Night was asked the same question.

"Not yet, Father Loon, but I seem to see a grayness before me."

When the lake had been crossed for the third time, the voice again asked, "Has the light come?"

"Yes, Father Loon, I can now see, though dimly."

Again the loon warned the medicine man to hold on tightly and again it dived. Once more the water flowed swiftly against the open eyes of Dark Night.

When the loon asked the question for the fourth time, the medicine man stood on the spot from where he had first heard the loud laugh of the loon. When he looked down, he clearly saw a great loon floating feather-light on the surface of the lake directly in front of him. Dark Night flung his arms skyward, hand held high, in heartfelt thanks.

"Father Loon," he gasped, his voice choked with joy, "I can see! How can I thank you? How can I ever repay you?" Then, swift as the swoop of a hawk, he knew. He would give the loon his greatest treasure, his sacred necklace. Fumbling fingers at last loosened the precious collar. With both trembling hands outstretched, he dropped the band of glistening white shells over the loon's head. As it raised its neck, the shimmering, snowy collar glided down its jet-black feathers. Like a lovely necklace it shone on the bird's neck. Some shells fell from the collar and lay sparkling on the loon's black back and wings. The bird raised its long black beak skyward. Four times its lilting laugh filled the twilight with music of savage splendor.

The heart of the medicine man was glad when he saw that his lovely collar of shells had become a gleaming necklace of glistening feathers, white as feathery flakes of snow.

✳ ✳ ✳

Walking Buffalo

Stoney

Here begins a folktale of mystery and magic, told today by the weavers of tales of the Stoney Indians of Alberta, Canada, most of whom believe that it is founded on fact.

Long ago, and yet not so very long ago, a big herd of bison—or buffalo, as these huge animals are popularly called—was grazing peacefully on the prairie, not far from what is now named the Bow River. The Rocky Mountains towered in the background. A great white wolf circled the herd closely, but neither the great guard bulls nor the cows, many with small calves drinking from their mothers, showed any alarm at its presence.

Something else seemed odd on the prairie that night, as the buffalo herd grazed and slept under the radiant stars. A strange, tiny creature, by far the smallest thing among them, moved uncertainly in the midst of the buffalo herd. The little thing crawled, then walked unsteadily under the belly of a buffalo cow. Giving little snorts and strange cries, and holding onto the hairy hind leg of a cow for support,

it pushed close to a tiny bull buffalo calf and drank, as noisily as the calf, the milk of the mother cow. Coyotes howled in the distance, and at times the great white wolf raised its head in a loud, quavering wail.

There had been a stir in the tepee camp of the Stoney Indians late that afternoon. Warriors, women of the tribe, and children, were looking for something. They searched everywhere and everything: inside the tepees, under skins and bushes, and in the long grass nearby. They found nothing.

A chief questioned a woman who wailed loudly outside a gaily colored tepee, surrounded by other women of the tribe. Between wails, the woman and her companions told the same story. Only a short time before, the little lost boy, wearing a buckskin shirt and moccasins, had been rolling on the grass, wrestling with mongrel dogs just outside the tepee of his grandmother. Then he had vanished! He was so young that he walked with difficulty and moved chiefly by crawling; so the people of the tribe asked, "How could he disappear so suddenly from the middle of so big a camp?"

That there was mystery, perhaps magic, in the thing, both the chiefs and the people agreed after they had searched the wooded areas near the camp, all of the following day.

That night, chiefs and a medicine man held a council fire, and the tribe gathered in a big circle around it. The medicine man, in full regalia and wearing a headdress of the wings of crows, raised his hands for silence. Arms outstretched in the attitude of prayer, he commanded that all sing to the Great Spirit, asking for the return of the little lost boy. He asked the chiefs and old men of the tribe to smoke their pipes, so that the prayers for the safety and return of the lost child would be carried upward to the Great Spirit. Then the medicine man cried out in a loud voice, asking if the boy was alive, and if so, where he was now.

Only the crisp crackle of sparks could be heard, as the medicine man awaited the answer. The wind rose softly and sighed gently, in the woods outside the council fire area. Suddenly the wind rose to a loud howl, which sounded like a human voice. The medicine man bent double and writhed for a moment, then leapt into the air. "The Great Spirit has spoken," he shouted. "The voice said, 'The boy will be found alive, with the buffalo herd.'"

Since there were many herds of buffalo roaming the vast plains, the medicine man prayed for a sign which would guide the search party to the right herd. The medicine man waited, with bowed head. Suddenly he gazed upward into the starry sky, scanning it with his keen eyes. "The buffalo herd which we seek feeds in the east," he declared. "A blue star tells me so."

Next morning, just after darkness had left to let the sun come, a big party of mounted Stoneys left the camp and rode eastward. They traveled all day and part of the night, without sighting buffalo. Next morning, and the next, they rode off again, before buffalo were sighted by the keen-eyed scouts. But these herds grazed to the north and south of the band of Stoneys; so, led by the medicine men, they continued riding to the east. Each passing day brought them deeper into enemy Blackfoot territory. Night shadows were darkening the land when the Stoneys saw a big herd of buffalo moving slowly eastward. The chief of the band decided that it had grown too dark to try to surround the herd in the hope of finding the lost boy, so they camped for the night, sending out four scouts to keep the buffalo herd in sight, without causing it alarm. The Stoneys knew that the buffalo would move only a short distance after dark.

When the first faint streaks of morning light shone in the east, two of the scouts returned. With a scout at each end of the long line of horsemen, the Stoneys cantered forward, side by side. They knew that the buffalo were not alarmed by men on horseback, provided the riders moved in silence and kept at some distance from the herd. Soon, the line of horsemen surrounded the lumbering herd, and the riders in front of the moving buffalo slowed their horses, to stop the slow advance of the herd.

When the hunt chiefs saw the size of the herd, they redoubled their efforts not to stampede the buffalo. Gradually closing in on the herd, a chief, riding beside the father of the boy, saw the little boy playing with the calves. Overcome with joy and forgetting caution, the happy father shouted to his son. His voice startled the animals; and, tails in air, they stampeded. Only one cow remained. Close beside her was a little bull calf and the boy who, instead of crawling toward his own people, tried to follow the buffalo herd. The buffalo cow, who showed no fear of the Indians, trotted after him and blocked his way, until his father picked the child up and held him tightly. Then she ran off to rejoin the running herd.

The child snorted and struggled to leave his father and follow the herd, which he seemed to regard as his own family. Knowing that the child had spent several days enjoying the family life of a baby buffalo and that, even in that brief time, the little boy might have become like a buffalo in thought, the medicine man decided to hold a council fire at once. When the Stoneys were seated around the medicine fire, which had been lit with sweet grass and on which medicine herbs smoldered, the medicine man talked to the child and sang a medicine song, while holding the boy tightly in his arms. Smoldering herbs were held under the nose of the child and a lock of his hair was burned with ceremony in the medicine fire. As though by magic, the little body became limp and, uttering a few baby words, the child stretched out his arms toward his father.

The search party returned in triumph to the Stoney encampment; and a great feast was held to celebrate the recovery of the little boy from the buffalo.

Later, a spirit dream was to come to this child, when he grew older: he spoke with a big buffalo bull which gave him advice. Still later, when he had become a young man, he followed the commands of his spirit totem animal and carried out his dream vision. He made a buffalo-skin tepee, painted it yellow with ochre paint, then painted on the tepee cover a range of hills, with a row of tepees in front of the hills, sheltered by them and facing west. A circle, which he painted on the cover, represented the sun. Finally, his name, Walking Buffalo, was depicted on the tepee in the form of a walking buffalo. This totem gave him strength and the power to lead and heal.*

✳ ✳ ✳

How Glooscap Made the Birds

Micmac

Long ago, there lived in the Land of Night a great giant known as Wolf-Wind. He was much feared by the Micmac because he brought

---

* Walking Buffalo, whose Indian name was Tatanga Mani, was a modern medicine man and chief of the Stoney Indians. He gained world-wide fame for his noble character, medicine power, and skill. He was born in 1871 and died in 1967.

When the author of this book visited with Walking Buffalo at Banff, Alberta, during Banff Indian Days just following the Calgary Stampede in the 1960s, the old chief was still living in his famous yellow tepee, at the Stoney encampment there. His headdress and his staff were each decorated with two upright buffalo horns, and his buffalo totem still gave him the power to heal and lead, in spite of his ninety-odd years.

trouble and sorrow wherever he went. He lived in the huge cave of the winds, in the Land of Night. He stayed inside when the countryside was very still and the sun blazed down, and on calm nights. He disliked calm seas and sunshine but greatly liked high winds and storm. When he came out of his cave, the very ground trembled and giant trees split and fell. Little trees and flowers tried to hide, but Wolf-Wind could move as silently as a shadow when he wanted to, so the plants and animals had no time to escape destruction. He blew the sea into great waves which were dashed to pieces on the rocks, and everything died when he was on the warpath. Whenever the cruel giant howled, when darkness covered the earth like a huge black blanket, fear spread throughout the land.

There were Indian villages close to the sea and the men and women fished, often far from shore, for their winter food supply. Their little fishing canoes floated like leaves on still waters, and the children played happily on the sandy beach while the sun shone. Then suddenly at sundown, Wolf-Wind rushed raging out of the north; the wind blew; the storm shrieked; great waves piled up in the sea and crashed on the shore, so that those who fished were drowned. The giant howled in rage and became more and more angry as his temper fed on the storm which he had raised.

Wolf-Wind was still raging when morning came and when he saw the children on the beach, looking for their parents. He churned through the rough sea to reach them, but before he could reach the shore, the children had fled in terror. They hid in a big cave and rolled boulders into its entrance to keep the giant out. He could not enter the cave and though he blew and howled outside it throughout the day and night, the boulders blocked his way. At last he stormed away, threatening to catch the children later.

The children were so terrified that they stayed in the cave until hunger forced them to go outside to look for food. They knew that their parents must have been drowned in the storm which had also destroyed their homes. The children heard Wolf-Wind howling in the distance, so they ran swiftly into a huge forest where they thought they would be safe. In the great forest, which the Indians knew as Willow Land, there were huge trees thickly covered with leaves, which would hide them from view if the giant came. The forest was a pleasant place where little streams flowed and flowers grew in little glades where the sun shone through.

Then, one day when the sun did not shine and the forest was very still, Wolf-Wind suddenly came again, bringing destruction with him. He raged through the forest searching for the children, but they were hidden from his sight by the thick leaves of the trees and bushes. Wolf-Wind raged into the distance, but from time to time he returned suddenly and swiftly in the hope of catching the children off guard. Sometimes some of them were off guard, but again and again they were screened by the protecting leaves. Only the sun in the summer-land country, far to the south, knew where the children were.

The giant became more and more furious and he began to be as angry with the sheltering trees as he was with the children whom they protected. He thought of another giant who could help him punish the trees, and went in search of him. When the leaves of many trees were beginning to wear gay shades of yellow and red, Wolf-Wind returned and with him the other giant who had a very powerful charm called the charm of frost. With this magic, he was able to make the leaves die and fall from the trees. Now, with Wolf-Wind blowing and raging, together they tried to strip the branches quite bare. Though most of the leaves came floating down, the efforts of the two giants had no effect on the evergreen trees such as pines and cedars; and the leaves of the alder, maple, oak, birch, and willow still clung to their branches. Wolf-Wind raged again because the children were still screened by their friends the leaves. "Wait," he growled. "Wait!"

One night, when the harvest moon shone high in the sky, the giants returned. This time their attack left only the leaves of the evergreen trees, which never lose their leaves, and the children moved under them for protection. The forest grew sad and still as so many naked trees shivered in the cold wind. Snow would soon come to the forest and it stood without even the whisper of a leaf to break the silence.

In those days, Glooscap was a powerful magician and ruler in the land of the Micmac Indians. He was a great maker of magic and each year he gave gifts to the children throughout the wide land of the Micmacs. Snow had fallen before the gift-giving day arrived, so Glooscap travelled in a splendid sled pulled by his huge, faithful companions, his dogs. When he arrived at a village, he asked the children what gifts they would like most. Because of his great power, he was known as "The Magic Master of Gifts," and he was always able to grant the wishes of children. His magic powers told him of the children who were hiding in the forest and he went to ask what their wishes were.

The sad children asked nothing for themselves, but they did beg the magician to bring back to life the leaves which had saved them from Wolf-Wind and return them to their trees.

Glooscap sat and thought for a long, long time. What the unselfish children asked for was big and powerful magic. In those days, there were only sea birds, such as gulls, ducks, and cranes, because Glooscap had not yet made any small land birds, and Wolf-Wind had no power over these sea birds. He had tried to harm them but they only laughed and mocked him, imitating his wild howls of rage when he could neither reach nor hurt them. There were also birds, such as the hen and turkey, which lived in some Indian villages.

As the magician thought very hard, a great idea came into his mind. The birds which he had made so far had rather unpleasant cries, so bird-song was unknown in the land of the Micmacs. When the children of the forest had spoken of "floating leaves," Glooscap had thought of floating birds, small ones, which could sing sweetly and wear brightly-colored coats of feathers. In the magic mirror of his mind, he could see red birds, blue birds, and many-colored birds singing cheerfully in the woods, fields, and villages, to make children and grown-ups happy.

Glooscap told the children that even his magic could not put the leaves which had been destroyed back onto the trees, but he could do something even more wonderful. He could change the leaves into little wings of the air, birds, which would always remember how they were born and know that they were related to the trees. In autumn, they would fly with summer to the land of summer-flowers, far away in the south. Then, when spring came, they would return to visit and live and nest among the tree branches from which they had come. All of the little feathered things would love the trees, the laughing brooks, the grass and the flowers, and they would sing sweet songs for the children. They would float in the air at times, so that they would remember they were related to the leaves; and the children would remember how they had been protected by the leaves from the power of the giants, and they would love the birds and protect them from harm.

Glooscap promised the children to give the trees, which Wolf-Wind had made bare, power to grow new leaves each spring, so they would be beautiful when summer came. The magician also promised to take away some of Wolf-Wind's power so that he would be unable to hurt the children any more.

Then Glooscap waved his magic wand, and the children were astonished and happy to see hundreds of beautiful little birds of all colors rise from the ground, where the fallen leaves had lain, and fly onto the branches of trees and bushes. The birds twittered and sang joyfully and many of them were the colors the leaves had been. The thrush and robin and other birds were colored shades of brown and red, like the oak leaves; the yellow birds were colored as the leaves of the birch and beech had been; and many other birds had been brightly colored by the magician, so that their feathers shone with blue and green, and purple and gray. The bird chorus was so sweet that the children were happy again.

Since it was very cold, because winter ruled the land, Glooscap sent nearly all of the little birds to the land of summer flowers until the cold months had gone. Then the little songsters returned to build their nests among the leaves, which sheltered them as the other leaves had sheltered the children. The little birds awoke the children in the morning with their sweet songs and at night their twittering and sleep songs put the children to sleep.

Even today the birds sing, because they have never forgotten that they were the special gift of Glooscap to the children, and that they were born from the leaves which had been torn from the trees so long ago.

*   *   *

The Swan Headdress

Northwest Coast

When the world was young, there lived a powerful medicine man who was known as a transformer, because of his power to change things as he willed. One day, he stood on the shore of a big lake in the Northwest coast territory, watching an Indian family in a canoe trying to catch some swans. They tried many times to catch the big birds but could not. Then the family paddled to shore. There was a father, daughter, and two sons in the canoe.

The sons knew that the medicine man was a transformer. They said, "Our father is old. He wishes a blanket and headdress of swan feathers, but we cannot catch the birds."

The medicine man took some swan feathers which the daughter held in her hand. He swiftly made a headdress for himself which looked like the head and neck of a swan. Then he took a long length of strong buckskin thong from his medicine bag.

Putting on the headdress, the medicine man swam out to where a flock of eight swans had landed on the lake. They looked at him but saw only a swan's neck and head above water, and thought he was another swan. He dived under the flock and swiftly fastened the buckskin thong around the birds' legs. Then he swam back to shore and tied the end of his line to a tree. He took off his swan headdress. The birds tried to fly away but they could not, so the family went out in the canoe and captured all of the swans.

When the Indians returned, they praised the medicine man and begged him to catch some more swans.

Though he should have known better, the medicine man was flattered by their praise. Once more, he swam out toward another flock

of eight swans. Again the great white birds showed no fear, and floated close together while the medicine man fastened his thong to their black legs.

When the medicine man neared shore, he tied the rope round his waist so that he might have his hands free to remove the swan headdress. When he took off the headdress in the water, he lost his magic power. The swans flew high into the sky. The medicine man loosened the thong from around his waist and hung onto it with his hands. Soon it cut so deeply into his fingers that he was forced to let go. He fell from so high, onto a great rock, that today the Indians still point out the hole he made when he landed.

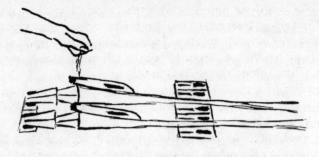

The Chant of Beauty
Navajo

The Navajo Teller of Tales tells it in this way. Bear, Frog, Snake and
Turtle decided to raid a village of people which lay beneath the ocean.
In the house of the shaman, it was said, were many magic things.
Since Bear and Snake could not swim under water, they kept watch on
the shore while the raid was taking place. Frog and Turtle rushed into
one of the hogans, the House of Shells, in the hope of capturing some
girls to take back to the shore, but the villagers heard the girls scream
and ran to their rescue. The people were so quick that the two raiders
knew that they could not capture any girls, so they scalped two of
them. The hair of the older girl was trimmed with white shells, and the
hair of the younger girl was adorned with turquoise. The raiders hid
the scalps in a medicine pouch and fled from the hogan.

The people attacked the theives so savagely that Frog, through a
magic power, shrank until he was so small that he was able to hide
under the shell of Turtle. They were both safe from attack then, since
even the strongest hammers and axes of the people of the village could
not break open the shell of Turtle. The people threw Turtle and Frog
into a great oven, where a hot fire was burning, hoping to burn them
to death. Frog wriggled out of the shell of Turtle and, making himself
much bigger, was able to squirt enough water onto the fire to put it
out.

Later, the villagers opened the door of the oven and found both
animals alive. As Frog and Turtle tried to escape, they were seized by
the people, who foolishly decided to drown the two raiders by throwing them into a swift river. It carried Turtle and Frog to safety, taking
the beautifully decorated scalps with them. When Frog and Turtle

came out of the river onto the shore, the wind blew along the coast and told Snake and Bear where to meet them.

As the four animals got close to their own village, they met eight villagers who wanted to know which of the raiders carried the two scalps, but none of the four would tell that secret.

Then two of the villagers, who had beautiful daughters, promised to give them as brides to the one who could shoot furthest. What the villagers really wanted to know was how strong the raiders were, so that they could take the jewels away from the thieves. The eight shot their arrows, then the others took turns. At first Bear and Snake would not agree to shoot because, they said, they were too old to compete against the younger men. Though some of the arrows went very far, none of them went as far as the shafts of Bear and Snake.

The younger men became very angry and rushed away toward the village, without waiting for Bear and Snake. Though they were older than the others, Bear and Snake soon caught up with the younger men and, once again, they held a bow shooting competition. Again Bear and Snake won, but the two villagers, whose daughters were to be the prizes, still would not give a true promise that they would be the brides of the raiders.

The party returned to the village, but Bear and Snake decided to camp a short distance from the village. They thought that the stolen treasure would be much safer that way. They built a comfortable shelter and planned a way to win the two daughters without any more competitions.

Back in the village, the people began to dance; and soon all the young people were dancing to the sound of drums and singing. As they danced, the two girls who were to have been prizes, began to smell a wonderful fragrance which seemed to call them. They decided to follow the scent trail and set off, without being noticed by the other dancers. The trail which they followed led them easily to the shelter which Bear and Snake had built. Looking in, they found, to their joy, two very handsome young men, richly clad. Bear-Man wore a rich black, while the clothes of Snake-Man had all of the rainbow colors woven into it. Both wore wonderful jewels, and were smiling kindly.

The elder of the two girls saw that the young men were smoking, and begged Bear for a little of the tobacco with the wonderful scent. He said, "No!" But Snake invited the two girls inside, telling them that they could try the tobacco inside. The girls liked the good looks and kind manners of the young men, so they entered the shelter and sat down. Bear gave his pipe of white shells to the elder girl; and Snake offered his beautiful turquoise pipe to the younger girl. Each girl took one puff on her pipe, then the world grew misty and black.

Next morning, Snake held strong incense under the noses of the girls, so that their senses returned. Then they saw that it was daylight and that Bear and Snake had become old men. That day the girls were kept prisoners, but when darkness came, the younger girl, Glispa, tried to escape. She knew that she was tied to the ankle of Snake by a thin, long, blue racer snake. It awoke from sleep each time she tried to loosen the knot from around her wrist. She waited until the blue racer slept again. Then, wetting her slim wrist with saliva, she managed to slip her hand through the small loop, without disturbing the snake which held her prisoner.

When she reached the door, she found that the shelter was surrounded by hundreds of hissing serpents. They hissed and threatened loudest when she was afraid; so she asked her spirits for courage. Then she was able to pass between the squirming snakes, to freedom.

But other great dangers awaited her. She had gone only a little distance from the shelter when she heard angry voices which she knew. Her relatives and friends from the village were searching for her. She knew that if they found her, they would kill her. Looking for a way to escape, she looked back over her shoulder, and saw that Snake was pursuing her. Fear gave her fast feet, and she raced to a nearby river and waded downstream, so that she would not leave a scent trail which Snake could follow.

She had nearly reached the mountains, and was circling the foot of one of them, when she became very thirsty. Suddenly a lake appeared directly in front of her. Then Snake People appeared and demanded from where she had come. She told them the truth about all that had happened and saw their hard faces soften. They raised one corner of the lake, as though it were made of buckskin, and told her that, because she had told them the truth, she might enter their country.

As she walked through a corn field, she ate, and people gave her water to drink and were kind to her. They took her into an adobe house, the same as the Pueblo people lived in, and told her that she would be quite safe from the old man from whom she had fled. She stayed in the house, and they fed her with magic cornmeal, from a magic bowl which never became empty. She went with her new friends to a great feast, where she saw the Snake-Man again; but she was not afraid of him, because once again he was young and handsome and dressed in splendid clothes of rainbow colors, as before.

She was happy, sat beside the young man while they feasted, and noted that all of the people who passed by greeted the young man respectfully. He told her that he was a powerful shaman, one of the very few to know the whole of the beautiful Hozoni chant; and also how to paint the magic, ritual sand-pictures, which were a part of the ceremony. It was a chant of healing.

When the girl said that she was very fond of music, the young man taught her the chant and painting. She learned these things very quickly. She was happy with the Snake People and stayed in their country two winters. Then she became homesick for her own people, and she told the Snake-Man magician of her feelings. She said that not only did she want to see her people, but that she also wanted to teach the chant and painting to her elder brother, who would use the magic to heal the sick in her country.

When Glispa returned to her people, she found that time had healed the differences between them and that they were no more angry. They welcomed her as one who had been dead; and she started at once to teach her brother the wonderful chant and sand paintings, which were fresh in her memory. Her brother tried very hard to learn, but he could not remember the correct arrangement of the songs in the chant, nor the manner in which the colors of the sands must be arranged, to bring healing.

After trying for a long time to teach her brother the mysteries, one day she directed his hands over the sand painting, as she sang the chant, and placed one kernel of maize at each color, where the change must be made; she also marked where each song in the chant started, by placing four maize kernels at each of the points. These were left until daylight came, when she had her servants gather maize. While chanting some of the magic parts of the chant, she made this maize into a thick soup. After her brother had eaten some of it, he remembered the words and positions of the songs in the chant; and exactly how the sand painting was laid out; and the places for each color.

Glispa was glad, and she taught her brother all of the ceremonies sung as part of the chant. She also showed him how the feather prayer offerings must be made during the ceremony. Her brother now learned everything very quickly. He soon became a great shaman who knew not only how to heal the sick, but also how to teach other shamans, so they could carry out the powerful Chant of Beauty ceremony.

The Navajo people were glad because of the great magic ceremony which was brought into their lives. When this ceremony took place, it lasted for four days and four nights, and the people took baths, to be very clean for the ceremony. Just as the final part of the ceremony was ending, the chief shaman told of the possible return of the Snake-Man. The people knew that he had the power to take them to the terrible underworld; so when a shaman, disguised as the Snake-Man, suddenly appeared, the shock effect on the patient being treated was usually so great that the cure was almost certain.

✳ ✳ ✳

The Magic Feast
Cheyenne

The Cheyenne were related linguistically to the powerful Algonquin family, and the territory of the Cheyenne lay just west of the head-waters of the mighty Mississippi River, at the time of this story.

One day a large number of the Cheyenne people were gathered in the big camp circle because they were going to hold a festival of games. Though the people were near starvation, they were very brave and their spirits were kept high by the members of their Red Fox Society, the bravest of the brave who smiled in the face of danger and laughed in the face of death.

Two medicine men of the tribe were in their lodges, dressing in full regalia and painting themselves, in order to attend the games. Each medicine man took special pains to wear exactly the right clothing and apply the paint to his face and body, in the way that the

Indians were always told to do through dreams or while fasting in a lonely place.

When the two medicine men were dressed in full regalia, they met on the way to the chief's lodge. Both men were astonished and angry to see that the other wore exactly the same dress and was feathered and painted in exactly the same way as he.

"Why," demanded one of the medicine men, "are you dressed the same as I? Are you trying to steal my power, or do you mock me?"

The other medicine man replied, "It is you who imitate me. How did you learn to dress as I am now?"

"Last night, in a medicine dream, I went to the clear spring close to our camp and there, reflected in the water, I saw such dress as I now wear," explained the medicine man who had spoken first. "Every feather, bead, and paint symbol was as I now wear them."

"There is much mystery and medicine in what you tell me," said the other. "Last night, when the stars came, I too went to the spring and dreamed, and there too I learned to dress like this."

They argued as to which had the better right to wear the dress, and at last decided to go to the spring together and try to find out which of them had the greater right. They set out for the spring, and the people followed them, silently.

When they stood at the edge of the spring, each medicine man dared the other to enter the deep pool. Together they stepped into the water and sank out of the sight of the people who looked on.

The two medicine men sank slowly to the foot of the pool. There they saw a very old woman who appeared to live in the spring. "Why do you come, and what do you want?" she demanded shrilly.

Knowing well the bite of hunger, they replied together, "Our people starve. No food have we, and even our best hunters can find no animals."

The old woman looked at each medicine man keenly, then she gave each an empty wooden bowl. Into one she put some corn, and into the other some pemmican. They thanked her, then up through the water went the medicine men to their waiting people.

They returned to the camp in silence. There, the medicine men distributed the food among the starving people. Though all ate as much as they could, the bowls remained full and did not empty. So the people feasted and gave thanks to the Great Spirit.

The old people of the Cheyenne say that this is how corn and pemmican first came to their people.

* * *

The High Cranberry Bush

Cree

The Man-Who-Wanders was considered a great magician by the Cree
Indians. They thought that he could make ripe fruit grow when and
where he wished. The magician knew better but was wise enough not
to tell the people that they were wrong. Like many of his admirers, the
Man-Who-Wanders was very bright and very dull, very wise and very
foolish. Often he was most stupid when he was trying to show how
smart he was, but the people forgave him easily because he had a
good sense of humor and usually knew how to laugh at himself when
he made mistakes.

The magician was hungry and thirsty. As he sat on the bank of a
wide, clear river, he was shaping a strip of canoe birch bark into a
drinking cup. Suddenly he gave a cry of joy because directly in front
of him, on the surface of the river, great bunches of ripe, red cranberries were floating. Eagerly he jumped into the stream to gather the
juicy fruit, went down over his head, and came up gasping, without
one berry.

Today I am not wise, he thought. They are deep down in the clear
water and I must dive for them.

He was wearing only a breechclout and moccasins, so he dived deeply into the cool water, down, down, deeper and deeper. He passed surprised fish and startled a big turtle but found no cranberries. He came to the surface and when he had regained his breath he started to surface dive for the fruit. Determination was one of his good points. He never gave up easily. He dived and dived, stroking his way down again and again without reaching even one berry. Finally he climbed out very tired onto the bank of the stream, and lay down.

"I will rest awhile before I start diving again," he gasped, and turned over onto his back.

Then he saw something which made him laugh and splutter.

"Today you have a dark cloud over your mind," he told himself. "What an idiot you have been to dive for shadow berries."

The magician laughed again at his foolishness. He had suddenly seen that the cranberries hung in scarlet bunches on a big bush that overhung the river, and he had been diving into the river where only their reflection lay. Finally the thought of his stupidity began to annoy him, so he stood up and threw a few big stones into the water where the reflection of the berries seemed to mock him.

"So!" he cried. "That will teach you to trick me."

The river chuckled on its way as each splash the stones made leapt up into the face of the Man-Who-Wanders and made him splutter again.

As the old man was throwing the stones into the river, the cranberry bush decided to play a trick on him. The bush remembered how many tricks the magician had played on the birds, beasts, trees, and plants. Now, thought the bush, is my chance to get even.

The man was examining the cuts which the rough stones had made in his fingers, looked at the smiling ripples in the stream, and realized that he was the only one who had been hurt by his display of bad temper.

"Well," he told himself, "I will forget my troubles after I have eaten some of this good fruit." He reached up above his head to gather a handful of the tempting berries, then gasped. When his fingers almost touched the cranberries, the branches seemed to rise a little, just enough to keep the fruit beyond his reach.

"You must not try to match your magic against mine," he shouted in anger at the bush.

Once more he tried to pick some of the berries, but they were always just beyond the tips of his eager fingers. Now he became really angry and jumped up and down under the bush, shouting and clutching at the lowest branches. They still avoided his grasp, so he became angrier and angrier. He threw some big stones as hard as he could at the elusive berries. He managed to knock down only a few, but they were so squashed and juiceless that they were not fit to eat. As he scowled up at the brilliant berries he did get some juice—in his eye.

"Hear me!" he shouted. "From now on you will remain tall. I will not eat your berries and nobody else will ever like their taste. You will always be scraggy. You will be known from now on as high-bush cranberry, so that you will never be mistaken for your sweet little sister. Sour berries, I have spoken!"

Princess and Slave

Kwakiutl

Prince Food Giver was a great Kwakiutl chief and warrior. He was powerful and everybody obeyed him except his daughter. The princess often did things which she knew were wrong, though she had been told not to do them. Many times, her father had warned her of the danger of walking alone in the forest. "It is not the beasts that you need fear," he said, "but the evil spirits and bad people who hide in the dark shadows of the giant cedar trees."

"Beware of D'sonoqua, the Wild Woman of the Woods," the wise men of the tribe told her. "Some day, as you travel alone down dim forest trails, she will seize you."

She did!

For four suns, the princess was held a prisoner by D'sonoqua before a band of daring warriors was able to rescue her. They got into the house of the Wild Woman by moving a plank on the roof while she was away gathering berries. She returned just as the princess and the warriors were leaving the clearing in which the house of D'sonoqua stood. She chased them with wild shouts. They shot many arrows at the Wild Woman as they fled, but they failed to stop her. The magic of D'sonoqua failed to prevent the band from reaching their village.

When the Wild Woman of the Woods came to the edge of the village, and saw Chief Food Giver and his people armed and ready for battle, she made magic. At once, she became as big and strong as a young spruce tree. Arrows and clubs did not hurt her. She would have killed many of the people, had not a wise old shaman thought of a way to stop her. He ordered some of the warriors to cut their mouths and tongues and spit the blood onto D'sonoqua.

They did that, and D'sonoqua began to shrink to the size of a human. She howled with pain when the blood struck her. After the warriors spat their blood on her four times, the Wild Woman begged for mercy. When the people shouted, "Kill the witch!" she pleaded to become the slave of the prince and guard the young princess from all harm.

"Let her try to do what she asks," ordered the prince. "If her work displeases us, then we shall give her to you and you may do with her what you will." The people had to be content with that promise.

D'sonoqua worked very hard to please the prince and princess. She became very fond of the princess and made her a gift of the beautiful little hummingbird which she kept tied, by a strand of spider's web, in her long black hair. After that, she showed the prince and princess a wonderful dance which they had never seen before and which pleased them greatly. D'sonoqua taught them the dance and told them that they might keep it for themselves and she would dance it no more.

A warrior who was jealous of the regard which the princess showed for a slave woman took counsel with a shaman who had much magic power. They schemed to put an end to the Wild Woman of the Woods who had become such a willing slave. They wanted to destroy her magic and her power over the princess. For a long time they were not able to do what they had planned, for D'sonoqua had much power which they feared.

The young princess always dressed as a princess should, and she took great care of her looks. D'sonoqua watched as the princess plucked her eyebrows until they were shaped like the moon when it was new. "Please! Please, let me do so with my eyebrows," D'sonoqua pleaded.

The princess was amused and gave her slave permission. D'sonoqua had little skill, and her bushy eyebrows looked worse than before, after she had plucked many hairs out with a clam shell. She begged the princess to have a woman of the tribe shape her eyebrows in the same way as those of her mistress.

The princess agreed, but she could not find a woman in the tribe who dared try to do what the Wild Woman wished. They all feared to displease her with their work. At last the young warrior heard of the difficulty and, after being counseled by the shaman, declared that he could shape the eyebrows in the way D'sonoqua wished.

When he went to the house of the princess to do what he had promised, he said that he would use a sharp, stone knife, instead of a plucking shell. He told the princess and the slave that the knife had magic power in it and that the eyebrows would not grow again after he had cut them.

He spoke truly! Before he began, he told D'sonoqua to close her eyes tightly, lest he hurt them with the sharp blade. As soon as she did so, the warrior drove the knife into her brain and the Wild Woman of the Woods fell dead at his feet.

✳ ✳ ✳

Raven Tales

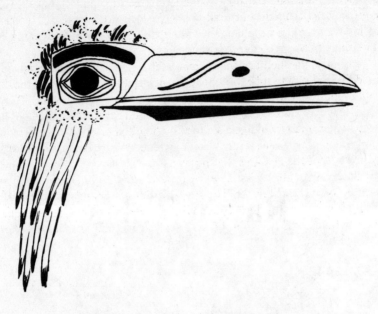

Black As a Raven

Bella Coola

Although Raven had caused the helpers of the Great Transformer much trouble, he was such a wise bird that he was sent down to earth, with transformer powers, to help men solve their difficulties. Sometimes he did this very well, but just as often he did not. Maybe that was because he was very wise and very foolish, very bright and very dull; and often he was most foolish when he was trying to show how bright he was. Sometimes as a raven, sometimes disguised as a human, he appears in many tales in this book which show what a strange old bird Raven, the trickster, really was.

When a Northwest Coast Indian says "black as a raven," he means "very, very black." The Bella Coola Indians tell this legend of why Raven is dark as the darkest night.

Raven was a very vain bird. Before sending Raven to earth, the Great Transformer told his helpers to make him the most colorful bird of all. They worked hard to obey their master's command, but the task proved too difficult. After many moons of labor, they thought that their work was well done. Raven was so beautifully colored that even the bluebird and the cardinal looked dull beside him. But each time Raven saw his reflection in a sky pool, he was not satisfied. He asked that his wing colors be changed. When that was done, he wanted his tail feathers to be given another shade.

Patiently the helpers made many changes. Still Raven was not pleased. The helpers told the Great Transformer of their difficulties, so he went out to the great workroom to see their handiwork. Raven looked like a rainbow, but he told the Great Transformer that he still thought that many changes should be made before he went down among men. The Great Transformer listened with patience while the big bird told of the changes that he wanted.

"Such a vain and dissatisfied bird deserves only one more change," said the Great Transformer. He gave a brief command to his helpers. They threw soot and ashes all over Raven until all of him was as black as night. Black was he when he was sent down among men, and he is still black today.

* * *

The Tide Woman

Haida

The Haida tell that the Tide Woman of the Great Inlet was always very busy. One of her duties was to control the tides of the Northwest

Coast. She did this by lying flat on her back and lifting her legs up and down. When they were up, high tide swirled around the rocks which were farthest up the beach. When the Tide Woman lowered her legs, the tide went out and the ocean no longer covered the beaches.

Not only did the Tide Woman work with the tides, through light and darkness, but she also had another hard task to take care of. It kept her arms and hands even busier than her feet and legs. She kept all fishes shut up in big magic boxes which were stored around her great house. Fish sometimes escaped from these boxes and were washed up onto the beach at high tide.

The Tide Woman was always very angry when fish escaped from the boxes, and she was in a great rage on the day K-Ka, the Raven, landed on the beach close to her house. As soon as Raven alighted, he transformed himself so that his wings, black coat, and beak disappeared and he became a man. He went to the door of the house of the Tide Woman and looked inside.

"Where have you been and what have you been doing?" the Tide Woman asked angrily, without changing her position or looking around to see who was there.

"I am very tired and very hungry, O woman of the tides," Raven said sadly. "I have been fishing for eulichan."

"You have not!" she cried angrily. "I have all of the eulichan safely in my boxes. Get out of my house and stay out!"

Raven was discouraged and went onto the beach and sat down on a big rock close to the ocean. He watched a gull swallow a dead eulichan before a nearby crane could seize the little fish. The fish gave Raven an idea. He only needed one of these little oily fish to carry out his plan. He watched each incoming wave eagerly but no more fish were washed ashore. To get what he wanted, he started a quarrel between the gull and the crane.

"Crane says that you have a big mouth and use it too much," he told the gull. The gull was very angry but did not dare to start a fight with a bird as big as the crane.

Raven walked over to the crane. "Sea gull says that you should keep your long nose out of other people's business," he told it.

With a loud, harsh cry, the crane ran over to the gull and kicked it so hard on its tail feathers that the fish which it had swallowed flew out of its mouth and fell on the beach close to Raven. Before the crane could reach it, Raven snatched up the oily little fish and rubbed it all over his hat. The smell of the fish was very strong.

Raven went back to the house of Tide Woman and stuck his head in through the doorway. The woman smelt the odor of fish at once and quickly turned her head toward Raven. "Where did you get the fish?" she asked sharply.

Raven patted his stomach, belched politely, and said slyly, "There are many, many fish in the ocean, not far from shore. There are far more fish there than you have in your magic boxes."

The Tide Woman wailed. "The fish are so slippery that they are always getting out of my boxes," she complained loudly.

"You are so busy with the tides that I often wonder why you try to take care of the fish too," Raven said. "Even a woman as clever as you has far more work than many men could do if they did nothing else but rule the tides. Why do you not throw all of the troublesome fish into the ocean?"

"That will I do," she exclaimed, jumping up so suddenly that she nearly knocked Raven out onto the beach. He took that chance to escape while the Tide Woman threw boxes and fish far out into the ocean.

It was because of this trick of Raven's that the Indians found so many different kinds of fish in the ocean from that time on.

✳ ✳ ✳

Raven, Canoe Builder

Tsimshian

After Raven had flown around the world, he landed in Tsimshian territory again, then took on human form. He was very tired after his long flights and the adventures he had met on the way. Above all, he was hungry, as always.

He saw smoke rising in the forest, and going in that direction he found a cabin sheltered among the tall trees. A beautiful young Tsimshian girl lived in the house with her mother, a widow, who proved to be very hospitable. There was much good food of all kinds stored in the house and after a huge meal Raven was in a mellow mood. He talked a lot, mostly about himself, not forgetting to tell how clever he was and boast of his ability, real and imaginary, to make things. An idea was being born in his fertile, tricky mind. "I will marry

your daughter, if you will let me have her," he told the widow, who readily agreed.

For several moons, Raven lived happily with his wife in the widow's house. When he sensed that his mother-in-law had at length begun to wonder why he did no real work, apart from eating, he turned to the trade which he knew best—trickery. One night he told his wife that he loved her so much that he was going to build a fine new canoe for her mother. He did not forget to add that, as he was a master craftsman, the canoe would be a thing of grace and beauty. So fine would the new canoe be, he assured her, that never again would they deign to use the old craft.

"Tell your dear mother—" Here, Raven was overcome for a moment, as he thought of his mother-in-law's skill as a cook, "that I will go into the forest soon after tomorrow's sun comes and look for a red cedar tree worthy of becoming her canoe. With the next sun will I fell and begin to shape a log from the tree which I have chosen." The daughter proudly carried Raven's message to her mother, who received it joyfully.

Next morning, after a huge breakfast, Raven told the women that he was off into the surrounding forest on a quest for the right tree for the canoe. He did go deep into the forest, rested until the sun began to hide between the trees, and then returned to his wife. After a supper even bigger than usual because, he explained, his appetite had been whetted by his search for the canoe tree, he told the women that after seeing many trees, he had found exactly the one for the purpose.

He assured the women that early next morning he would be off into the forest again to cut down the tree and start work on it. His wife was eager for him to do so, especially since he had told her what a happy time they would have in the wonderful, new canoe. A natural storyteller, he painted a glowing word-picture of the near future, when they would paddle swiftly around the nearby islands with his wife in the stern, her mother amidship, and himself in the bow. Next morning, almost before darkness had gone, he left for the forest to begin his task. He took along not only a huge breakfast which his mother-in-law had made him and which he had devoured like a wolf, but also much food to sustain him during the day's work, and his mother-in-law's stone tools.

When the heat of the day had passed, the women heard the purposeful thud of the axe, deep in the forest. After a while, there was the sound of a tree crashing to the forest floor. Apparently Raven did not cease work even then. The listeners heard the resounding blows of the axe continuing. The master canoe builder, they thought, must have begun the difficult task of hollowing out the log. When darkness came, Raven dragged himself wearily into the house, tired out by his work on the canoe, he told them. He sat down to a huge feast which the two women had prepared. Apparently Raven's weariness did not affect his appetite, which caused his mother-in-law to glance toward the fast-emptying storage boxes. That night, Raven asked his wife to suggest to her mother that a big dried salmon, boiled especially for him each night, would supply the sort of nourishment needed by a canoe builder.

After four more days of toil, Raven announced at salmon supper time that the canoe would soon be finished. "Soon" stretched into many days and at last the mother said to her daughter, "Go secretly into the forest. Follow the sounds of the axe until they guide you to your canoe builder. See how near the canoe is to being finished. Return quickly and tell me without letting your husband know. Often master builders do not like a woman to look on their work before it is finished."

The daughter obeyed her mother and followed the sound trail with some difficulty, because the axe had spoken less and less as the days passed. When the young woman approached cautiously the place where the canoe builder was at work, she stopped and watched him from behind a great cedar log. Raven had just climbed onto a bough bed of cedar branches and now lay happily on his back singing a little song which builders of canoes sing when at work. Raven did not neglect his work either. From time to time, he dragged himself from his bed and gave an old cedar log, which lay nearby, a few gentle strokes with the back of the axe head. A hole in the end of the half-rotten log echoed and made greater the sounds so that, from a distance, one would readily imagine that a man was hard at work.

Silent as a wisp of wood smoke, the wife faded into the forest. When she reached home, she shamefacedly told her mother how the work on the new canoe was progressing.

That night, the canoe builder returned home dog-tired but happy at the thought of the fine meal awaiting him.

Happiness died within him as he pushed open the heavy cedar door of the house. Everything had vanished, the food boxes, his beautiful wife, and his bountiful mother-in-law. He rushed out of the house to the water's edge where the old canoe had been moored. It was gone. He realized that the women had returned to their tribe.

Raven was sad, very sad, because he was very hungry.

* * *

Raven and Fog Woman
Northwest Coast

When the world was very young, Raven and two of his slaves were fishing in a great bay on the Northwest Coast, in the hope of catching some salmon. They could catch only bullheads, so Raven and his helpers began to paddle toward their camp at the mouth of the creek. Soon their canoe was swallowed up in a thick fog and it was impossible to see the length of a paddle blade in front of them. Suddenly the fog lifted a little, and Raven and his slaves were surprised to see a woman sitting in the middle of their canoe. She asked Raven to give her his spruce-root hat. She took it in her left hand and held it in front of her. Immediately, all of the fog streamed into the hat and they were able to paddle to camp without difficulty.

Raven knew that the woman had shaman power so he married her. One day Raven started out on a fishing trip, leaving one of his slaves in camp with Fog Woman, which was the name he had given his wife. When Raven was gone a long time, Fog Woman became hungry and asked the slave to fill a water basket at the spring and bring it to her. When he did so, she dipped a finger into the water, then told the slave to empty the basket toward the ocean. He did so, and a big salmon came splashing out with the water. She told the slave to club the fish, so that it would not suffer for long, and cook it at once before her husband returned. After feasting on the salmon, she ordered the slave to clean his teeth thoroughly so that Raven would not

know what they had eaten. She warned the slave not to mention the salmon.

When Raven returned, the slave ran to meet him. The man looked so contented that Raven demanded to know what had happened while he was away. The slave assured him that nothing had happened but Raven frightened him into telling about the salmon-which-came-from-nowhere.

Raven went to Fog Woman and asked her where the salmon really came from. Because of her love for her husband, Fog Woman told him her secret. She asked him to fill his hat full of water at the spring and bring it to her. Raven did so gladly because he had been unlucky on his fishing trip and was very hungry. As soon as Raven brought in the hatful of water, his wife dipped four fingers into it, and when he emptied the water out, four fine sockeye salmon flopped on the ground where the water fell. The slave killed and cooked all four, and Raven and his wife feasted and sang.

Just as soon as they had finished feasting, Raven asked Fog Woman if she could conjure up more great fish like the ones they had just eaten, for these were the first sockeye salmon that he had ever seen. She told him that she had the power to do so, but first he would have to build a smoke-house with many racks, before she would make the salmon come.

Raven soon built a big smokehouse and gladly obeyed Fog Woman when she told him to bring her a big basket full of water. She washed her hair in the basket and told Raven to empty the water into the spring from which he had brought it. He did so, and at once the spring teemed with splendid sockeyes. Raven and his slaves caught and cleaned many salmon and hung them on the racks in the smoke-house to dry. There were enough salmon in the spring to fill three smokehouses.

Raven was happy to think of the fine food supply for the winter, but after a while he scolded his wife about things. They argued and the quick-tempered Raven struck Fog Woman. She told him that she would leave at once and return to her father's house. At first he did not believe her. She brushed her hair and, as she did so, a sound like the rushing of wind and water came from the direction of the smokehouse.

Fog Woman walked quietly from the house toward the ocean and the noise of rushing winds became louder and seemed to follow her. When she had almost reached the water, Raven ran after her and begged her to remain, but she said nothing as she walked ever nearer to the ocean. Raven tried to catch her but his hands passed through her as they would have passed through fog.

Then Raven howled in sorrow. At last he knew what caused the strange wind-like noise. All of the salmon, even the smoked and dried ones on the racks, were following Fog Woman onto the beach. Raven and his two slaves tried to catch some of the salmon but they could not hold onto them. Slowly all of the sockeyes disappeared with Fog Woman into the ocean. Raven had only a few bullheads to eat during the long winter. Even with his most powerful magic, Raven could not bring either Fog Woman or the salmon back.

Since then, Creek Woman, the daughter of Fog Woman, calls the fish up the streams from the ocean.

✳ ✳ ✳

How Raven Got the Salmon
Northwest Coast

As soon as Raven heard about the wonderful salmon-fish, he wanted to get some so that they would spawn in the great rivers of his land. Then he was told by a spirit-person that Beaver had all the salmon, which he guarded very carefully.

Raven tried a few clever ruses to make the old beaver part with a few salmon, but he was never able to get any. Then, using his transformer powers, he hit upon a way to get what he wanted. He turned himself into a good-looking boy, and visited Beaver in his lodge.

At first, the old chief would not allow the disguised Raven even to look inside the lodge. Raven told him that he was a poor orphan boy with no friends, and hardly enough food to keep him alive. He added that he would be glad to help Beaver with his work, simply for food and to have a roof over his head.

Raven then shared the lodge with Beaver and did everything he could to make the old chief less suspicious. At first, when Beaver went fishing for salmon, he always left Raven shut up in the lodge. But after a time, he let the young man wander freely.

One night, after a fine salmon feast, Raven asked Beaver where he caught such wonderful fish. "I have a river and lake, with many salmon in them," the old chief replied. "But they are all mine; and nobody can have even one of them."

After that, Raven worked harder and harder for Beaver, until Beaver trusted him well enough to take him salmon fishing. The boy proved a clever fisherman; and after a while, Beaver let him go fishing by himself. During these fishing trips, Raven managed to steal quite a few fine salmon, and he placed them in a cool, hidden, little lake.

One day, Raven had enough salmon to stock some rivers and lakes. While old Beaver slept, Raven transformed himself into a huge raven and flew off with the precious fish. He placed them in suitable lakes and rivers; and they multiplied so quickly, that soon the Indians of the Northwest Coast had all the salmon they could eat.

❋ ❋ ❋

Raven and Fish Woman
Haida

Raven, the transformer, was hungry. He was often hungry, since transforming things was hard work and the legends of the Haida tell that Raven was perhaps the hungriest of all who made magic. On this day, he decided to go out in his canoe and catch fish. Out on the ocean, Raven caught many fish, but they leapt out of the canoe just as soon as he laid them on the bottom of his dugout. This angered the transformer, who had hoped for a quick feast.

With an idea in his mind, Raven paddled quickly to shore. He found a spruce tree and collected a big handful of spruce gum. Quickly he molded it into the shape of a woman. "Now, grow fast and fat," he ordered. The woman obeyed.

Raven took her out in his canoe. She sat in the stern, while he sat in the middle of the canoe and fished. Each time he caught a fish, he threw it behind him and told the woman to sit on it so that it could not jump back into the ocean.

The sun blazed in the sky and Raven caught fish and threw them back to his helper without looking around. His one idea was to catch as many fish as he could in the shortest time and then paddle back to shore and the welcome shade of the forest.

The woman made so little noise that Raven called out in Chinook jargon, "Kla howya? (How are you?)" from time to time. At first, she answered "Klosh! (Fine!)" but her voice was very faint and it seemed to grow more and more faint. Soon she only said, "Ohh," in reply, then there was complete silence.

Raven turned around to see what was the matter when the woman no longer replied to his questions. She was gone. So were all

the fish except a small one with bulging eyes, on account of the weight of the woman who had sat on it, and a patch of black spruce pitch on its topside. The underside was white, but Raven would not eat a fish with the remains of the spruce woman on top of it, so he angrily threw it back into the ocean.

Today, the halibut still has bulging eyes and the black marking on one side. The Indians, remembering the adventures of Raven, always carry a halibut club with which to knock each halibut on the head as soon as it is pulled into the canoe.

✳ ✳ ✳

Raven and the Dancer

Haida

"At last, I must build a canoe," Raven told himself. In his lazy, human form, the trickster was slowly trying to paddle a very old canoe, leaking from many poorly patched holes, into the mouth of a Haida creek which flowed into the ocean. It was a very long time since Raven had built a canoe, because for many moons he had been able to beg or borrow one, and when he could not do so, he was nearly always clever enough to find a canoe which was nearly built and almost ready to put into the water.

Wet to the waist, Raven managed to scramble ashore. He heard the sound of a drum being beaten in the forest and knew that a village of some sort was not far away. Now, Raven scouted carefully along the shore which skirted the great cedar forest for miles. He was looking for an easy-to-come-by canoe, but could find none.

At last Raven gave up his search and, selecting a spot on shore where the ocean came closest to the forest, he ate a hearty meal, then started to chop and burn down a suitable cedar that would make a canoe the size he needed. He worked hard on the canoe-to-be, gradually shaping and hollowing out the log so that, with the help of a smoldering charcoal and ash fire, he could burn the remaining wood from the inside of the canoe. He could launch it later, with the aid of a few villagers. Raven knew that he would have to work on the burning-out process for a day or two. For once he worked steadily, refusing the many invitations of the honored but suspicious people of the village to consider their village his.

The wife of the village chief was especially nice to Raven and kept telling him of a pretty and clever dancer who was going to dance at the village in two nights. Not only did she paint a picture of the dance that set Raven thinking, but she sent her two boys to mention the dance and dancer when they went to watch Raven working on his canoe. "Chiefs and many people come from everywhere," they assured Raven. "Nobody wants to miss her performance. Our mother says that she will keep a place of honor for you right beside where this beautiful woman will dance."

"Tell her that I will not be there. I must watch by my canoe. It should be ready by tomorrow, when darkness comes," said Raven. When the boys had gone, he packed more smoldering charcoal around the inside gunwales of his canoe-to-be and lay down beside it to wait until morning came. Late the next day, he saw that there was still quite a bit of burning to be done before the sides of the canoe would be charred to the right thickness. He worked steadily on the posts for the bow and stern, though the sounds of drums and song from the village tempted him greatly when darkness came.

At times, Raven's powerful imagination caused him to see the dancer, slim, beautiful, and luminous, dancing enticingly on the shore to the rhythm of the mind-music which he provided. When this maiden-of-his-mind passed close to him, as she glided into the forest in the direction of the village, he followed her. When he arrived at the great house, he saw that the real dancer was just going to begin. Raven was led to the seat of honor and some eagle down was ceremoniously sprinkled over him as he sat down. Then the dance began.

Raven's eyes became big and round as he watched the pretty dancer step and turn and move sinuously to the cadence of the drums and rhythm boards. For a long time she danced, but the passing of time went unnoticed to Raven. When the dancer seemed to pause for even a moment, the onlookers thumped their sticks and staves on the floor, and the dancer spun with even greater agility than before.

The night had almost gone when Raven started out on the trail which led through the great cedar forest to the shore. He was in a daze until he reached the spot where his canoe should have been. Then suddenly, he became fully awake. Thieves must have stolen his canoe, he thought. Then the truth hit him like a thunderbolt, as he saw only a few planks and posts smoldering on the sand. The shout that he gave was heard in the village. The people had been waiting for it! While he had watched the dancer, the unchecked fire had done its work too well. The planks and posts that were visible were all that remained of his canoe.

* * *

Raven and the Shadow People
Haida

Raven was flying slowly over the stormy water of the Hecate Strait when he saw a Haida village far below. Seeing a chance for possible mischief, he landed on the beach. The transformer took the form of a man as soon as he alighted close to some other ravens looking for tidbits on the shore. Raven thought himself so clever that he never suspected that keen eyes were watching him from the village. Although he did not know it, he was about to match his wits against the Shadow People.

Raven walked slowly up the wide rocky beach. His tender feet, unused to walking on such a rough surface, became cut by the many mussel shells and bruised by the rocks and stones. He thought for a moment of transforming again, taking wing and landing closer to the village, but decided it was unwise to do so, as someone might see either his transformation from human to raven or from raven to human. He headed toward a large house built of red cedar planks. It looked like the house of a chief. Voices inside the dwelling whispered, "That trickster Raven is coming. Let us guard against his cunning tricks."

Raven entered the huge house and was surprised to see everything so well arranged. The roof planks had been stacked so that the rays of the sun brightened every corner of the dwelling. He was even more astonished to find nobody in or around the house. There were all sorts of foods stored in the house. Edible roots, barks, and berries were neatly piled on shelves, and dried salmon and halibut hung from hooks, ready to be taken down and eaten. "This looks like a place where even a transformer might be happy, especially if he were left alone to satisfy his taste for good food," thought Raven.

Though Raven was not hungry, he decided to have a feast after he had satisfied his curiosity by taking a good look at everything in the house. As he moved from place to place, he was startled to notice a dark shadow following him. He hurried as fast as his aching feet would let him, then walked so slowly that he hardly moved, but the shadow never left him. He struck downward at it. The black shape did not move, and he heard giggling nearby.

Raven went back to the rack on which the fish hung and took down a big red salmon. He looked around for a place where he could eat the fish in comfort. He found a beautifully carved red cedar chest covered with soft sea-otter skins, on a raised platform which was always the resting place of a chief. He laid the salmon down beside him while he looked at his injured feet. Then he reached for the fish. It was gone!

Raven had been using his mind a great deal on his work of transformation, so he could not decide whether he was imagining things or whether he was being deceived by some strange, powerful magic. He went back to the fish rack and took down another fine salmon. This time he laid it within easy reach, and decided to keep his eye on it for a moment or two before beginning the feast. He had wondered during the past moon whether his mind was weakening or his will power lessening. He closed his eyes for a second so that he could concentrate more easily on this matter, which was troubling him greatly. When he opened his eyes, his salmon was gone!

Once more, Raven returned to the rack. Once more, he chose a fine salmon. Once more, he returned to the seat of the chief to enjoy the fish in comfort. He laid it between his legs and kept his hand on it as he looked cautiously around. A dark shadow moved on the floor in front of him. With a wild cry of rage, Raven took his hand from the fish and jumped angrily on the shadow. The kicking and jumping had done his weary feet no good, but at least the shadow had disappeared. With a sigh, he reached for the salmon. It was no longer there!

Again Raven hobbled to the rack on which the tempting treasures hung. This time, he did not unhook a salmon because, to his amazement, the three fine salmon which he had chosen were again hanging on the hooks from which he had taken them.

Raven knew when he was beaten. He limped to the door, with the shadow close behind him, and changed swiftly into bird form. He flew away, leaving the shadow behind. Yes, Raven reflected, his magic was not as strong a medicine as he had supposed it to be before his experience in the village of the Shadow People.

✳ ✳ ✳

Romance
and Enchantment

Team

Micmac

Long, long ago, a great chief, warrior, and magician named Team, lived in the country of the Micmacs. He was a great friend of Glooscap, who was also a powerful maker of magic; but one great power which his friend Team possessed, Glosscap could not equal. Team could make himself invisible so he could listen unseen to the scheming of their enemies. He lived near the Atlantic Ocean with his sister, who helped him in his work. Many were the maidens who were eager to marry Team, but he had said that he would marry only the one who had the power to see him when he returned home, after the blanket of darkness had covered the land. Many had tried, but all had failed in the test.

Each day, when the sun left to let the moon come, Team's sister walked along the beach to meet him, and any maiden who hoped to become the wife of Team could walk with his sister to take the test. Only his sister could see him when he returned home after nightfall, and she would ask the maiden if she could see Team. Most of them replied falsely, pretending that they could see Team when they could not; then his sister would ask with what he drew his great sled along.

In reply, the maidens said that he drew his sled with a strong cord, or moose-hide thongs, or a pole, and his sister knew that they were only guessing. Team would not marry any of them.

A great chief of a nearby village had three daughters. Their mother had been dead a long time. The youngest daughter was not only beautiful, she was also good-hearted and gentle, so that she was loved by the people of her father's village. The other two sisters were very jealous of their young sister and the fact that she was so popular with all whom she met. The two sisters cut off her beautiful long hair, made scars on her face with hot coals, and forced her to wear very old clothes, hoping that this would make her ugly. They told their father that she had injured herself and, because their young sister was too sweet and patient to tell their father how she had received her injuries, he never knew what was really happening, though he often wondered.

The two older sisters made up their minds to win Team. One day, they walked along the shore with his sister at dusk, to await his return home. When Team's sister saw him coming, she asked the two girls if they could see him. They both declared that they could, very well. When his sister asked what his shoulder straps were made of, they both guessed and said, "Rawhide." Team knew that they had spoken falsely, so he let them see only his coat and moccasins when he took them off, but they could not see him. They were both afraid and amazed, and hurried away without saying one word.

After a long time, the youngest sister thought that she should try to see Team. She repaired her old clothes and wore the few poor ornaments which she had, and tried to leave without her sisters seeing her, but they did. They laughed at her and mocked her and tried to discourage her, but she had made up her mind and she went. The people who had learned what she was about to do felt sorry for her because they felt that she would have little chance, or none at all, after so many other girls had failed.

When night came, Team's sister, who had been very kind to the girl, walked along the beach with her, as they went to meet Team. As he came into sight, his sister asked the young girl if she could see him, and she replied sadly, "No."

Team's sister was pleased with the girl's honest reply and asked her again if she could see him now. The startled maiden answered, "Yes, oh yes! He is very wonderful!"

Team's sister then asked what Team drew his sled with, and the girl replied, "The rainbow."

"What is his bowstring made of?" Team's sister asked.

"The Milky Way," the astonished girl replied.

"Truly, you have seen my brother," said Team's sister. She knew that Team had made himself visible to the girl because she had spoken the truth when she had said "No."

Team's sister took the girl home with her, bathed her face scars so that they disappeared, and rubbed a magic oil on her hair so that it grew longer than ever before. Then she dressed the girl in beautiful clothes, gave her lovely ornaments, and led her to the seat of the bride. Then Team came in and sat beside her. She became his wife and helped him in his work, and they were very happy.

Team changed the two cruel sisters into aspen trees, and even today they still shiver and whisper, so that the Indians call them "the Trees-That-Talk-to-Themselves."

* * *

The Blackfoot Lovers
Blackfoot

One day, three warriors in full regalia galloped to the tepee of an old chief, in a Blackfoot encampment. They told the chief that they had come from a far distant village, to ask for his three beautiful daughters in marriage.

The old chief was glad, when he looked at the three braves who wished to become his sons-in-law. They were tall, straight, and rode their fine horses with great skill.

The young men told the chief that they had heard of the great beauty and skills of the three maidens and were prepared to offer whatever the old chief desired, before becoming his sons-in-law.

The old chief was not only wise but also brave; and he asked for something which would prove not only the generosity of the three suitors but also their bravery. "When you return to my encampment together," he said, "each of you shall drive before him twenty fine ponies, taken from the villages of your enemies."

The young men realized that this offering was not too great for such beautiful and talented young women.

The old chief had the three girls feast with their suitors in his great tepee, that night; and all of the young men were willing, had they been asked, to bring an extra five ponies as an offering to the father of such lovely maidens.

Before they rode away, when the moon rode high in the sky, the young suitors told the chief and his daughters that it might be many moons before they returned together to claim their brides, since fine ponies were always well guarded; and it would be difficult to capture more than one pony at a time, perhaps two, from different Indian bands spread over a large territory. Also, some of them might be wounded by the enemy, and would have to recover enough to ride and raid again, before carrying off more ponies. The chief knew that their words were true; and the girls promised to have patience as they awaited the return of the young warriors.

Many moons passed, and then more. There was great wailing from the women of the Blackfoot encampment. The chief painted his face as a sign of mourning, and sat alone with heavy heart in his tepee. The three maidens had waited patiently for many moons; and when more and more had come and gone, the girls decided to wait no longer. They decided that their husbands-to-be had been killed; and the brave girls had decided to meet them in the spirit world. So, together they leaped from a high cliff, into the rocky gorge behind their encampment.

Not long after, three warriors in high spirits drove sixty fine ponies ahead of them, as they rode fast toward the Blackfoot encampment. Because of the passing of so many moons, they were eager to see their wives-to-be.

Good fortune and bad fortune had ridden with the young men on their raids. There had been fights, wounds, loss of captive ponies—

recaptured by their owners, in some cases—but now all was well, and they galloped, driving their captured trophies hard in front of them.

The encampment lay only a little distance ahead of them, and now they awaited the coming of mounted warriors, who would ride out from the camp to welcome them. Then, as they came closer to the Blackfoot encampment, they heard the loud wails of the women of the tribe; and they rode together to the lodge of the chief, where they learned the sad tidings.

The broken-hearted braves decided at once to rejoin the women of their choice in the spirit land. They galloped to the edge of the great cliff, which towered over the rocky ravine far below; and, dismounting, they leaped together onto the rocks beneath.

✳ ✳ ✳

Konakadet

Haida

A highborn young man who had many good qualities married the daughter of a great Haida chief. The chief's wife had not wished her daughter to marry the man because he was known to be a gambler. She became a nagging mother-in-law who made difficulties for her son-in-law whenever possible. She ordered her slaves to put the fire out as soon as she had eaten, so that the young man could not cook a meal for himself when he got up late in the day. Being the wife of an important chief, the mother-in-law was angry because she could not dominate the young man as she did so many others, including her daughter. When the son-in-law entered the community house late at night after hours of gambling, the chief's wife would say mockingly, "My noble son-in-law has been gathering wood for me," or "He has been fishing so that I shall have salmon for my table."

Tired of the constant sarcasm and nagging, the young man built himself a little red cedar cabin on the shore of a big lake, beside the ocean. He knew that the water monster, Konakadet, was said to live in the lake. One day he saw it swimming far out, and watched until it dived under the bank close to a great tree which had fallen into the water.

The young man was brave and made preparations to trap the huge monster, which was believed to possess magic powers. He split the trunk of the tree, far down under the water, and forced the two sides apart with strong levers. Then he held them open with a strong wooden trigger, so that when it was knocked out, the two sides of the trap would snap together as if with a giant spring. He tempted the monster into the trap by using a lure baited with salmon. He cleverly decoyed the monster so close to the trigger that, when it lunged for the bait, it knocked the trigger out from between the jaws of the trap. The powerful beast fought furiously to escape but the great tree held it a prisoner until it drowned.

The youth then skinned Konakadet, carefully scraped and prepared the skin, and slipped into it. The monster-magic seemed to remain in the skin because its new wearer found himself quite comfortable inside it. Far more wonderful, he had inherited the magic hunting power and strength of the monster and was able to swim, dive, and hunt in the deepest and roughest water. He dived to the bottom of the lake where he found a beautiful dwelling of hewn cedar logs which had belonged to the water monster.

The young man found a big, hollow tree close to the edge of the lake where he cleverly hid the skin of the monster. He told only his wife of trapping the monster and of his new magical powers. He pledged her to keep what he had told her a complete secret from everyone. She promised and her word was good.

When spring came, the people of the little village had used up all of the dried foods. Times were hard because fishing was bad and the hunters had little luck in the forest.

One evening, the young man said to his wife, "Tonight I go fishing in my magic skin. In the morning I must return before the big raven croaks, but should you hear its call before I get back, seek me not, for I shall be dead."

That night he caught a huge salmon. Very early next morning, he laid it high up on the beach in front of the house of his mother-in-law. She found it there but thought it had drifted in to her on the tide. As the wife of a chief, custom demanded that she share the fish with high ranking villagers. The following morning, two great salmon lay close to her door. "A spirit must be helping me!" she exclaimed, and shared the fish with hungry villagers.

The son-in-law, tired after his underwater adventures, now slept most of the day. His mother-in-law mocked and chided him. "A man should not sleep all day in time of famine. Did I not have the good fortune to find dead fish on the beach, we would starve," she complained.

Next morning, before the sun rose, a big halibut flapped on the beach before her door. Believing that spirits must be aiding her, she predicted, in the presence of a group of villagers who were admiring the great fish, "Tomorrow will I have two halibut, instead of one."

Her son-in-law heard her boast and as she had proclaimed, next morning two halibut lay on the beach. This caused the mother-in-law to become prouder and more arrogant than before. She asked her husband the chief to allow nobody on the beach each morning before she had visited it. Her unusual request was made, she said, as a result of a vision. The chief, not knowing that the wily woman wanted to be certain that anything washed onto the beach would be claimed by her first, ordered that nobody be permitted to go down onto the beach each morning before his wife did.

Since signs seemed favorable, the mother-in-law next prophesied that she would be sent a seal. Next morning, a big seal was lying on the beach. As the hungry villagers feasted, the woman proclaimed herself a powerful shaman. In the circumstances, nobody doubted her boastful words and neither chief nor shaman disputed her claim.

She had a fine headdress made, such as was worn only by shamans, as well as an apron, adorned with the beaks of puffins, and a beautifully carved mask. This, with great ceremony, she named "Food Finding Spirit." All ranks of villagers now fully believed in her spirit power and she increased their belief by her "spirit" songs and dances. Public praise made her still more haughty and demanding than ever and now she always spoke mockingly of her son-in-law as "the man who sleeps."

The daughter, who was ashamed of her mother's brazen conduct, knew it to be most unfair to her husband. She asked him why he permitted her mother to make the false claims and take credit for his hunting prowess.

"Some day, her lies will catch up with her," he answered, "and the false shaman will be shamed before all the village. That will be punishment enough. Meanwhile, I gain skill, strength, and endurance, as I hunt and as I feel my magic powers becoming greater."

His wife was comforted by his words and said no more, except to warn him that one day the raven might croak before he had finished his task.

As the days passed, the woman "shaman" became bolder in her demands. She asked for sea lions and whales. One at a time, her "spirit" duly delivered them. She now sold the food which came ashore and became very rich. One morning, the young man remembered his wife's warning words when he got a whale beached only a moment before the hoarse call of the raven came from just overhead.

"Do not take any food from your mother unless she offers it to you," he told his wife before he left that night, "and if, some morning, I am found dead in the skin of the monster, put both me and the skin in the hollow tree where I used to hide it."

The time came when the mother-in-law, eager to display her power before the people of the village, predicted that two whales would be found on the beach next morning. Throughout the night, before the fingers of dawn streaked the sky with gray, the young man struggled with all his spirit and bodily power to beach two whales which he had caught. He had just dragged them both clear of the ocean and started to pull them high on the beach, when he heard wings above him and the raven's harsh *kak-kak-kak*.

The mother-in-law found the two whales, with a strange monster lying dead between them. The villagers flocked down to the beach to see the strange beast. It had a huge head with wolf-like ears, a great, scale-covered body with two big fins rising from its back, a long, curving tail, and great curved claws, which looked like copper. The villagers thought the monster must be the woman shaman's helper until the chief's daughter ran down to the beach and threw herself on the monster, calling it "husband" and bewailing his death.

She turned fiercely on her mother and demanded, "Where are your spirit helpers now? You lied, and lied when you declared you were helped by spirits. Spirits do not die. If this is one of your spirits, make it come alive again!" The villagers, who had crowded around, waited for the false shaman to reply, but she did not.

The young widow asked a chief who stood nearby to help her open the monster's mouth. When this was done, her dead husband was seen inside. "Konakadet must have eaten him," cried the villagers. They helped the sorrowful wife carry the dead man and the monster's skin to the lake shore and put them into the big hollow tree. Then they saw the trap in which Konakadet had been caught. They guessed the truth and wept at the death of the young man who had saved them all from starvation.

The villagers returned to the mother-in-law's house and mocked and shamed her with the knowledge that they knew all. She ran from them, shaking and quivering, and died in convulsions on the beach beside the dead whales.

Each evening, the unhappy wife went to the hollow tree to mourn for her husband. Then, one evening, she saw ripples on the lake. They came toward her, and to her surprise and joy, Konakadet rose to the surface.

"Climb onto my back and hold on tightly," a voice told her. She obeyed the voice because it was that of her husband, and rode down to the beautiful dwelling at the bottom of the lake.

She and her husband lived there happily and their many daughters came to be known as the "Daughters of the Creek." These spirit maidens live at the source of streams and those who see one of them, or their spirit parents, always have much luck.

❋ ❋ ❋

The Serpent of the Sea

Zuni

Long, long ago, in the village of K'iakime, or Home of the Eagles, which lay at the foot of Thunder Mountain in the land of the Zuni, lived the daughter of the chief priest of the village. She was a beautiful maiden who loved cleanliness more than anything else. She could not endure dirt of any kind and she often bathed in the "Pool of the Apaches," which the people of the Pueblo knew was considered sacred by the powerful Serpent of the Sea, named Kólowissi. Because of his great magic powers, the serpent knew that the maiden was leaving dirt in the sacred waters of the spring and he thought of a way not only to stop the maiden but also to punish her.

The next time the maiden came to bathe in the spring, she was astonished to see a beautiful little child splashing and laughing in the cool, clear water. The child was really the serpent, a magician, who by his magic could take many shapes and forms. Had the maiden known, she would have run for safety to the house of her father, the priest. She could not imagine where such a young child had come from and her keen eyes looked to the north, south, east, and west in search of a parent or someone who might have brought the happy child to the spring. Since she saw no one, she thought that the child must have been deserted by a cruel mother who had left her child to the mercy of strangers. "Poor little child," said the maiden. "I will take it to my house and take care of it."

The maiden took the child into her arms and spoke softly to it. She then carried it up the hill to her house. She climbed up the wooden ladder which led to the room in which she lived and laid the young child on a pile of blankets. The room of the maiden was high up in the dwelling and set apart from the other rooms because she could not bear the dust and dirt which was in the other rooms.

Forgetful of time, the maiden played with the child which laughed and cooed and rolled joyfully in the blankets. She had come to love the child and her heart was glad.

In the meantime, the other sisters had cooked the evening meal and had everything ready for the return of their elder sister. As the time passed, they wondered where she could be. They would have been more anxious still had not their old father said that she was no doubt still at the spring, washing clothes and bathing. He sent one of his daughters to the spring to call her.

When the younger daughter saw that her sister was not at the spring, she hurried back to the house and climbed the ladder leading to the room of her elder sister. Looking through the doorway, she was astonished to see her sister playing happily with a strange child. She hurried back to tell her father what she had seen. The other girls wanted to run and see the child but the old priest sat silent in thought. He knew that the spring was sacred and he feared that a magic spell possessed his daughter. The father ordered his other daughters to remain with him. He told them that no mother would leave her child in the spring and he feared that there was a deeper meaning in the mystery than they imagined. The daughters called to their sister to come down to the meal, but she did not even answer.

After a while, the child became sleepy and the maiden placed it on a bed. She lay down beside it and soon they both seemed fast asleep. The maiden slept soundly, but the child only pretended to be sleepy so that magic might be worked. The child grew longer and longer until, as though in some horrible nightmare, it became a great serpent. Its huge coils spread around the room until it was filled with great, gleaming, scaly circles. Placing its head close to that of the sleeping maiden, the serpent then folded her within its coils and ended by taking its tail into its mouth.

When the night had gone to let day come, breakfast was made ready, but still the elder sister did not reply to the calls of her sisters.

Though the old father said that no doubt his daughter thought of nothing but the child and they should breakfast without her, curiosity made the youngest sister run up to the room and knock on the door. When no answer came, she tried to push the door open but it would not move. Frightened, she ran to the skyhole in the ceiling of the room in which she had left her family, and cried loudly for help. All except the old father ran to the bedroom door and pushed with all their might. They were able to open the door about the width of a finger and, peering through, they saw the great, gleaming coils of the serpent. The women rushed screaming to their father. He ordered them to be silent and then told them that, as he had first feared, great magic had come to their home, but it was possible that he, as priest and wise man, could do something to break the spell.

The old man, troubled and angry over the folly of his eldest daughter, then went to the door of her room. He pushed against the door and spoke to the Serpent of the Sea. He begged the serpent to let the daughter return to her father so that he could atone for her wrongs. He said that he knew that because she had been taken captive by the serpent she belonged to it and she would have to return to it. Once again, the priest promised the serpent his daughter in marriage, and he continued to beg forgiveness for himself and his daughter.

As the priest prayed, the great serpent loosened his coils, causing the entire building to shake violently. So great was the shock that the villagers trembled. Awakened by the shock, the maiden cried loudly to her father for help. She begged him to release her from the spell of the serpent-monster. As the coils loosened, she was able to stand up. Then the huge serpent raised his folds nearest the door, so that an arch formed. Filled with fear, because of the great rasping noise and the sight of the huge coils, the girl dashed beneath the arch, out of the room and into the arms of her terrified mother.

When the priest had once again promised the serpent that the maiden would be given to him, the old man called the two warrior-priests of the town and they called a solemn council of all the other priests. Together they performed the sacred ceremonies in preparation for a marriage, gathering together the plumes, prayer wands, and treasure offerings. Four days of toil passed before everything was ready and consecrated to the Serpent of the Sea. On the morning when all was ready, the old priest sent for his daughter and told her to prepare herself to be given, along with all of the other treasure offerings, to the Serpent of the Sea and Spring. He also warned her that from then onward she must forget about her home, her family, and the Pueblo people, and live in the domain of the great Serpent of the

Spring and Sea. The priest sadly pointed out that she must have had the wish to become the bride of the serpent, since she had constantly angered him by defiling the waters of his spring, and she must get ready at once to join him.

With tears and in fear, she left her weeping family and the house where she had been born. In the plaza, all was ready for the preparation of the "bride of the serpent," as the villagers called her. While the people wept, they dressed the maiden in the ceremonial robes of cotton, richly embroidered and decorated, placed bracelets on her arms and earrings in her ears, and gave her beads and many rich and precious gifts. They painted crimson circles on her cheeks and sprinkled a road, which led toward the doorway of the Serpent of the Sea, with sacred meal. Then, at the western end of the plaza, leading toward the sacred doorway, they dug four steps in the form of a sacred terrace, leading toward the sacred spring.

Dressed in his full regalia as chief priest, the father of the girl then instructed her to stand on the terrace and tell the serpent that she was ready. Slowly, the door of the house of the serpent opened, and from the high room the serpent uncoiled and lowered his huge neck and head to the ground where the maiden stood trembling. The serpent placed his head gently on her shoulder and the priests solemnly chanted, "It is time." Then the serpent writhed slowly toward the west, gently guiding the girl and supporting her when she staggered from the path.

And so they went slowly toward the trail by the river and passed over the Mountain of the Red Paint, and still the great length of the serpent was not uncoiled from the room of the house from which he had descended. The strange pair had reached the foot of the mountain on the other side before all of the body of the serpent was on the ground. Here, the body of the serpent began to change. It contracted and became shorter and shorter, and gradually took on the form of a human being. The girl was afraid to look over her shoulder or she would have been astonished at the great magic change which was taking place behind her. Soon the serpent lifted his head from her shoulder and the dreaded form changed into that of a handsome young man, wonderfully dressed in sacred ceremonial robes. He gathered together the shrunken serpent scales under his cloak and called to the maiden in a voice which was a hiss, asking her to speak with him. Terrified, the maiden trudged wearily onward with her eyes turned downward. Several times, he asked her if she was tired, and his voice became softer each time he spoke. At last, hearing the now gentle voice ask her if she were weary, she turned around gradually to see the person who seemed to speak to her from a distance. The weight of the head of the serpent still seemed to press on her shoulder, because she had carried it so far, and it was difficult to turn around even slowly. When she managed to do so, she was amazed and glad to see a very handsome young man, dressed in the magnificent robes of a great chief, standing close behind her.

"May I walk beside you?" he asked gently. "And why do you not speak to me?"

"Because I am full of fear, and shame, and misery," she replied.

"Why do you feel so?" he asked. "Of what have you fear?"

"I am afraid because I came to this place with a dreadful creature which rested its head on my shoulder. I can still feel its great weight," she said, raising her hand to her shoulder.

"Strange," the smiling youth replied. "I have been with you all the time and I have seen no such creature."

"I know that you must speak truly," she said, "so where has the terrible thing gone?"

"I know where he has gone," answered the young man.

"Will he let me be now, so that I may return in peace to the village of my people?" she asked eagerly.

"No, that he will not do, because he is too fond of you," the youth answered.

"How can that be, and where has he gone?" she questioned.

"He has not gone; he is here. I am he," he answered, placing his hand on his heart as a sign that he spoke truthfully.

"You are truly he?" asked the maiden.

In reply, the young man pulled the shrunken serpent scales from inside his flowing robe, and the maiden was glad to see that what had been a serpent was now a gentle human being whose eyes told her that he cared.

"I love you," he said simply, letting his eyes speak for him. "You must come with me, and we shall dwell happily forever in the waters of the spring, which are also the waters of the world."

Side by side, they travelled on. She forgot that she had been sad and afraid and even forgot her old home. And so, together they reached the doorway of the Serpent of the Sea and went down into his magic home, where they dwelt happily ever after.

Ever since that ancient time, the Indians have considered the waters of all springs their most precious gift, and use their waters even now for drinking only, and for no other purpose.

❋ ❋ ❋

The White Rock

Cowichan

"No," the chief of the Cowichans said firmly. "I will not give you my daughter, even though you are the son of a sea god. You know that your father also refuses his permission for the marriage. So must it be. I have spoken!"

The young sea god was sad. He wanted the beautiful daughter of the Cowichan chief more than any thing that he had ever wanted before. The father of the young man, a god of the sea, was friendly with the Cowichan people and helped them when their canoes went to sea. In return, the Cowichan gave him many rich gifts.

In those days, long since gone by, the lodges of the Cowichan stood on the shore of what is now Vancouver Island in British Columbia, where the town of Sidney now stands. Knowing the will of their chief, the Cowichan were not friendly to the young sea god when he came to their village; and it was very difficult for the daughter of the chief to be alone with the young god-man who wished to marry her. But although the chief kept watch, the two young people were able to meet sometimes on the shore after night had fallen.

Though she loved the young man very much, the young woman of the tribe was afraid of her father. She was just as much afraid of what the young man, using his magic power, might do to her father and her tribe, if he were sent away. Because he truly loved the girl, he would not use his power to harm the tribe; so he thought of a way to win the girl, without losing the good will of the Cowichan.

After many moons, the chief of the Cowichan and his Wise Ones agreed to let the young man have the girl, if he threw a great white rock, which stood close to the edge of the sea, to a distant bay. "Even the son of a sea god cannot throw such a giant rock so far," the chief thought. But he did not know what the power of love, aided by the power of magic, could do!

So, early one morning as the sun rose, the chief, the wise men, and the tribe gathered on the beach behind the great white rock, and waited for the young man to do the impossible. The girl stood by the side of her father, and suddenly the time had come.

The young man stood beside the rock. It looked bigger than ever, compared with the slim young man. He saluted the chief and his daughter by raising his hand high, and then he crouched behind the big white rock. There was a sudden noise, as though a great wave had struck the rock; and when the young god-man stood straight up, the astonished people saw that he held the huge rock balanced high above his head. They saw the muscles of his arms and shoulders swell as though they would burst. They held their breath when they saw him bend his knees. "N'hhh," they murmured, when the young man straightened and threw the rock with a mighty forward heave.

The great white rock flew high and far toward a distant bay, which today is called Semiahmoo Bay. As the distance of flight increased, and the rock appeared to travel slower, everyone except the young man and the girl believed that the rock would not reach the shore of the bay. But love and magic combined, as often before in Indian legend. The great rock fell on the shore of the bay, across the wide strait.

The young man turned and went to the chief and his daughter. The stern face of the chief almost smiled, as the young man took the hand of the girl, and they walked together down to the beach. Here they launched a canoe, and paddled until an island hid them from view. They continued until they reached the mainland, where the great white rock had fallen, and decided to make their home in the beautiful country surrounding it. There they lived and founded the Semiahmoo tribe.

Though the passage of time could have wiped out all signs of such a feat, some deeds of old can still affect the present. Let us look at the legend of the white rock and its effect on the people of Sidney today. During a recent celebration in the town of White Rock, the Sidney delegation demanded the return of the White Rock to Sidney because, they argued, it had been thrown from there.

"Yes," agreed the citizens of White Rock, "but it landed here, and so it is ours, as it has been for all these many years."

Words became threats, and the delegation from Sidney left in a hurry, after first measuring the rock at Semiahmoo Bay. The Mayor of White Rock is still pondering a letter from the Mayor of Sidney, which officially demands the return of the White Rock. Because of this, the citizens of White Rock are keeping a sharp eye on the rock.

✳ ✳ ✳

The Lazy One

Northwest Coast

Sometimes when a canoe crew of Northwest Coast fishermen were very tired from paddling, these hardy fishers of huge fish would sit down, as the sun was leaving to let night come, and listen to the tales of one of their story tellers. The stories which they heard were about many things, and among them was usually one about a hero of their rugged coast. One of these stories was about a lazy boy, and the teller of tales usually told it in this way.

In a big village on the northwest coast lived a child who was so lazy that the villagers laughed at him. They mocked him and called him "the sleepy one," and other harder names. They did not know that he was favored by the Wise Ones and that he was preparing himself to be strong and great. They only knew that he lived in the great house of his uncle who was a chief, and that he slept most of the time.

When, as the boy grew older, the men and bigger boys of the village were far out on the stormy seas, fishing and hunting whales, the Lazy One would go to the ocean and bathe. He rubbed himself then with strange, powerful herbs which made him stronger and stronger. Nobody knew this, because he did these things in secret; nor did they know that he had a loon messenger, though they saw the great bird at times.

To deceive the people, this strange boy always pretended to be lazy and foolish when he was not asleep. Because of this, he was always the last person asked to help when big difficulties arose. When such times did come, the villagers could not help but see that this young-man-to-be had unusual strength and was clever. Some even said that he might be a spirit being, or even a transformer; but many others thought that this could not be.

Then came a time when nature seemed to threaten the lives of the people of the village. The forests and the mountains were slowly moving in on the villages further inland, and began to crush the houses and people there. Shamans and chiefs tried, by their magic powers, to stop the trees and mountains. Their magic was not strong enough, and at last they said that the only way to escape being destroyed was to take to their great canoes and put to sea, in search of new sites for their villages. Just before the people left, while the last canoe was being loaded, a good-hearted woman thought of the Lazy One and awakened him from a deep sleep. He sat up, saw the people seated in canoes, and asked what was happening. He went down to the canoes and a chief scolded him bitterly. "Maybe you could have helped your people," he said, "but you have slept so long and so hard that nobody could awaken you. While you slept, the moving forest has swept whole villages into the ocean."

When he heard these words, the young man rushed up the beach, hurried behind the great cedar houses, and pulled up great trees by their roots. These he built into a great barricade with which he pushed the threatening forest, bit by bit, far back from the village. Then he uprooted so many trees that he knew the forest would not be able to move toward the village again for many, many snows. He did this great work so quickly that he found the people still in their canoes when he returned to the edge of the beach. "If you have only little things like this to make you fear," he told the chief loudly, "you will have few real troubles."

Then he curled up like a tired dog before the ashes of a fire and fell asleep again, as though he had not been awakened.

Not many moons after this, the spirits which controlled the form of the earth began to flatten the mountains so that they became hills and joined each other. This was a terrible thing for the people of the village because they saw that the waters of the mighty rivers, behind the hills, would soon flow over the tops of the huge dam which the hills formed, and would sweep the village and all in it out into the ocean. Once again the villagers prepared to flee, but this time they told the Lazy One what was happening. He showed neither interest nor fear, and went to sleep again with a smile. But again the villagers shook him until he awakened and then the shamans told him of the great danger which threatened.

This time the young man went and looked at what had happened, and he knew that the Wise Ones were right and that something big had to be done at once. First he bathed, then he chewed some magic herbs until he felt great power within him. Now he called his loon, which acted as his messenger, and commanded it to fly fast to the grandfather of the young man and tell him what was happening. "Tell him that I must have great strength, so that I can push back the hills and break passages between them. The water, which is held prisoner, must flow past the villages to the ocean, leaving the villages untouched."

With a hoarse cry, the loon flew fast away. When night had gone and day came again, the young man heard the cries of the loon. They told him that his grandfather had heard and that the magic powers which the young man needed had been sent. The young man felt this great magic working in his body, and at once began tearing the hills apart, letting the waters escape where they could not cause floods in the village. Then the young man returned to the house of his uncle and slept again.

His people rejoiced and praised him as the greatest shaman in all the land. They felt great sorrow that they had ever mocked him, and they piled great gifts for him at the door of the house of his uncle. Then, one night, the sound of a great drum was heard far out on the ocean. The villagers rushed down onto the beach and looked out to sea. Soon, a great canoe with many men on board but nobody paddling it floated high up onto the beach. A tall man, wearing the rich clothing of a great chief, stepped from the canoe and told his servants, "This is where our master sleeps. We have come for him."

Then, followed by his servants, he walked at once to the house of the chief, the uncle of the young man. There the Lazy One lay sound asleep. He sat up as soon as the messengers entered the house and asked the chief why he had come. "Master, your grandfather the great chief is old and ill, and he has sent for you," answered the chief messenger. "He sends the message that you have done everything well, and that you have done all that was to be done. He said to tell you that your task here is done and that the magic canoe is here to take you home."

"I am ready," answered the young man simply. Then, turning to the village chief, his uncle, he said, "I must leave you now and return to my old grandfather who has grown weak. He is known as The-One-Who-Holds-Up-The-Earth, and I go to take his place on the pole which holds up the earth. You can be sure now that you will have no more big difficulties. Before I go, I have a message to give to your people. They must never again mock or make fun of anyone whom they do not know. To do so will bring much bad luck. Tell them to listen well when you give them my message. Now I must leave you." With these words, he led the way to the door. They went down the beach and went aboard the great canoe. When all were on board, it glided away into the darkness.

✳ ✳ ✳

Mystery and Magic

Death Calls a Hunter

Eskimo

Niviaksiak, hunter and greatest of Eskimo artists, thought too deeply and tried to pry into the mysteries of life. He spent months alone on a little island thinking about life, nature, and the animals. Wise men of his tribe and Indian tribes which camped nearby warned him that he searched too deeply into these things and told him that there are mysteries which are best left alone. But he heeded not.

A few years ago, he became obsessed with the great white bear, which he regarded as a beast of mystery. For months, he carved and drew studies of only the polar bear. Fellow hunters who passed his skin-covered workroom at dusk hastened their steps and declared that Niviaksiak's ivory polar bears swayed from side to side as night shadows fell.

One winter morning, Niviaksiak, who was an expert guide, led a small hunting party by boat to a primitive camp about forty miles north of Cape Dorset. That afternoon, the party returned to the place where it had disembarked and found that their skin boat had been torn apart. Niviaksiak and another hunter followed huge, fresh bear tracks which led from the boat. Suddenly, both hunters saw an enormous polar bear reared on its hind legs, towering above them. Niviaksiak, who was in the lead, raised his rifle—but he did not fire. He cried out, "Ah, it is dark! I am falling," and dropped onto the snow at the bear's feet. His fellow-hunter fled. Next morning, the hunting party returned to the spot of Niviaksiak's encounter with the great white bear. The hunter's body lay untouched where it had fallen. The tracks

(NOTE: The official record, dated 1966, states that Niviaksiak, artist-hunter, died while on a hunt, from a cause or causes unknown.)

of the bear ended on the spot where bear and hunter had met, face to face, the day before.

A white doctor searched for a medical clue to the cause of Niviaksiak's death, but the old, wise men of the Eskimo and the hunter who had fled knew—Niviaksiak had come too close to the life secrets of the great white bear. The hunter had been struck down by the spirits and their earthly instrument had then vanished.

✳ ✳ ✳

Maker of Rain

Squamish

The door of the great house of Si'atmulth, Maker of Rain, was not like the doors in the houses of the Squamish nobles and people. It had strange figures carved and painted on both sides. They were far different from any totem figures painted on other doors. There was a good reason for this: it was a magic door which helped its owner to make rain.

When the Maker of Rain pushed the door open just a little, light showers began to fall almost as soon as the door swung outward on its

leather hinges. When the door was opened a little wider, it rained
steadily. When Si'atmulth opened it wide, there was a downpour of
rain which nearly swept people off their feet.

The medicine man used his power wisely and the Squamish people had always enough rain to keep the soil soft and rich. The lakes
were always full and the rivers and streams always had plenty of
water for both the fish and the hungry earth, which drank greedily as
the clear, clean waters flowed past. Great cedars drank also, and the
huge, straight shafts raised their proud heads high. Flowers bloomed,
berries ripened, and the Squamish people were glad.

A great ceremonial potlatch changed all this. The medicine man
had hard words with Chief Kapalana, chief of all the Squamish. The
Rain Maker declared that he had not been shown enough honor at the
potlatch, where chiefs, medicine men, and nobles had gathered from
all along the coast. The other chiefs and nobles agreed with their tribal
chief, Kapalana. They too said that the Maker of Rain had been seated
and treated with all respect due to his position and power. When the
medicine man threatened to use his magic against them, they were not
greatly afraid. They thought that after the passing of a few suns, the
anger of the Maker of Rain would be less hot and he would forget. But
no, the Maker of Rain did not forget. When he reached his house, he
pulled the rain-making door so wide open that he was nearly washed
away by the downpour before he could get inside.

The Maker of Rain waited until darkness was almost gone, then
he nearly closed his door and listened. From the village, he heard the
sound of music and singing and knew that the people still feasted and
danced without thinking of his threats. More angry than before,
Si'atmulth thought hard. Then he smiled, for a bad thought had come
to him. He put on his medicine robe and mask and ran through the
forest until he reached the great house of Chief Kapalana. The guards
were afraid to stop him, and he bounded into the huge hall. He pulled
a cord so that his mask opened. When the merry-makers saw his rage-
filled face, the music stopped. They danced and sang no longer.

"Hear me," yelled the Maker of Rain, as he stood close to the
chiefs beside the fire. "There will be no more rain. My door will
remain shut, always!"

The medicine man ran from the house before Chief Kapalana
could have him stopped. When the Maker of Rain reached home, he
had his wife help him weave a long ladder of vines. This ladder could
be rolled from the smoke-hole in the high roof, over the edge of the
roof, down to the ground. It could be pulled up easily if anyone came.
The Maker of Rain made much magic, stored plenty of food and water

in his big house, then closed the rain door so that it could not be forced open from the outside.

For many suns, it did not rain. The people thought at first that the Maker of Rain would send rain when his anger had cooled, but he did not. Moons came and went. The sun-dried earth was brown and bare. Lakes, rivers, and streams became dry and the people suffered. The wife of Si'atmulth was sorry for the children of the people, because she had a young child of her own. She begged her husband to bring rain for the Squamish, but he would not.

Chief Kapalana called a council of chiefs and magic makers to decide what should be done. They went to the house of the Maker of Rain. Though they heard movements within, nobody replied to their shouts and pleading.

"Our people die of thirst!" shouted the chiefs, but the only reply was a loud, harsh laugh from the direction of the smoke-hole.

Even the magic makers were afraid to touch the magic door. Some chiefs said that they should cut through the strong cedar planks of the house with their heaviest axes and capture the medicine man.

Chief Kapalana, wiser than the rest, said, "No! When he hears us breaking down the wall, he may destroy his magic door from within. Then we can do nothing to make things right."

Then the magic makers and a secret society of young nobles of the Squamish had a big thought. "We know what is to be done," they told the tribal chief.

While the blazing sun shone on a burnt earth, the makers of magic used their mysterious powers which some wise men had in the days when the world was very young. They bathed, prayed, and worked spells, so that they might be ready to carry out their plan when darkness came. When it was dark, some of the makers of magic transformed themselves and members of the secret society into mosquitoes, and others became the terrible, tiny, stinging "no-seeums." They entered the house of the Maker of Rain through small openings in the roof. Soon, Si'atmulth and his wife were crying aloud in pain, as they struck blindly at these unseen enemies in the dark. Their child was not stung, and slept peacefully in its cradle.

While the Maker of Rain and his wife groped toward the nearly-dead fire to blow on the embers, from which they could quickly get light, the insects flew out of the house and returned to the village. Only two remained, invisible, on the high roof. When the Maker of Rain and his wife, weary and badly bitten, at last slept in deep sleep, the two insects flew down, said the four magic transforming words, and became young warriors again. They went softly to the cradle where the young child slept soundly. One warrior picked it up and carried it gently in his arms, while the other young man softly opened the rain-making door a little. They moved silently through the forest to a canoe which was waiting for them, and the paddlers drove it forward into the dark waters of the sound.

Later, when a strong wind blew the door of the Maker of Rain's house wide open, he and his wife were awakened by rain falling in torrents on the roof. The medicine man rushed to see why the door had opened, while his wife went to her baby's cradle. Her piteous screams alarmed the Maker of Rain.

"What has happened?" he shouted.

"My baby has gone," she cried as she ran to her husband.

A sad and frightened Maker of Rain, leaving his rain-door half open, ran through the dripping forest to the council house of his tribe. The chiefs expected him and were gathered in council when he arrived.

"Give us back our child," the Maker of Rain pleaded.

"Why should we do so?" asked the chiefs. "Your heart was of stone when our children suffered from thirst and hunger. Why should we feel pity for you and yours?"

The Maker of Rain wept and begged the chiefs to return his child, until the sun was high in the sky. "Only give us back our child and I will do all that you command, always," he promised.

At last the chiefs agreed to return the child, after the Maker of Rain had solemnly agreed to obey all of Chief Kapalana's commands.

Even today, when the Squamish in and around Vancouver, hear the patter of rain on the roofs, they say, "Si'atmulth keeps his promise."

✻ ✻ ✻

The Coming of the Thunderbird

Kwakiutl

A Kwakiutl chief and some of his people were trying to build a log house on the bank of a fast-flowing river. It was the first house they

had ever tried to build. They could not find a way to raise a long, heavy beam to hold up the roof. Each time they were able to place one end of the beam on top of a high post, it would roll off before they could raise the other end into place. They tried again and again but failed. They were sad and discouraged when they heard the beat of mighty wings high in the sky above them. A great black shadow fell on the Indians and a huge bird landed on the ground close to where they were standing.

The people were afraid and covered their eyes. Only the chief dared to look up when a shrill, mighty voice asked, "What do you?"

The chief saw that it was the great eagle-like bird which had spoken. "We are trying to build a house, O Mighty One," the chief replied, "but we cannot raise the big logs into their places. Maybe you are the great thunderbird that our grandfathers have told us of. Maybe you can help us with the work?"

"That I can do, and that is why I am here," the thunderbird answered. "What do you wish done?"

The chief pointed to the heavy beam which they could not raise onto the upright posts. With wing-beats so powerful that the Indians could hardly stand upright because of the strong wind which they made, the mighty bird flew up into the sky. He dived straight down onto the beam. The thunderbird seized the great log in his long, sharp talons, raised it high above the tall, upright posts, and placed it in position. Then he put other heavy beams into their places in the house. The grateful chief and his people thanked the thunderbird. When darkness came, the bird flew off into the night, after saying, "I will be your friend and keep watch over you."

The chief and his band rolled a giant stone to the spot where the thunderbird had landed. To this day, they call the village which they built there, "The Place Where the Thunderbird Came To Us," and the huge boulder is still pointed out by the Indians.

* * *

Magic Barriers
Haida

The sun shone brightly as a princess of the Haida set out to gather wild berries. She went alone, because she was without fear and did not wish to follow forest trails with chattering girls who would scare the birds and beasts away with their noise.

At first the princess found few berries, and went from thicket to thicket until she met a black bear. It was not unfriendly, for it had found and feasted on much honey. "Where may I find some berries, bear?" the young woman asked.

"Take these," he growled, pointing with his nose to some very dirty berries on the ground behind him. They did not look like berries to the princess and she told the bear that she would not touch such berries.

The bear became angry at her words and stood up in a threatening way, but three men came by and the bear shuffled off quickly into the forest. The men told the princess where she could find good berries. She thanked them and went in that direction.

The young woman found an old man picking berries when she arrived at the new patches. They picked the wild fruit together for a while. When their baskets were almost full, the princess noticed a movement in the bushes, on the other side of a clearing. She watched,

and her keen eyes saw the head of a bear among the branches. She was afraid, and told her companion what had happened before she met him.

The old man, who seemed to be wise and to have shaman power, was alarmed. "The bear feels that you insulted it," he told the princess, "and it has followed your trail to seek revenge. It is good that I possess power to help you to escape. Let us go fast to yonder stream, and fill our water baskets."

They went down to where clear water flowed fast and, after filling their baskets, the old man took some big pebbles from the edge of the stream before they hurried away. Soon they heard rustling in the bushes behind them, and saw that the bear was following fast on their trail. It came ever closer and its savage growls frightened the princess.

"Throw this stone backward over your head," said the old man, handing her a pebble. "Throw it but a little way. You will see what happens."

The princess did as the old man said. When she looked back over her shoulder, she was astonished to see that what had been flat country was now a high mountain. There was no sign of the bear.

"He is on the other side of the mountain," the old man told her, with a smile. "He will have to come around."

The bear took a long time to work its way around the barrier, but just before the sun was leaving to let night come, the princess heard the bear growling behind them.

"Throw a little of the water from your basket onto the ground behind you," said the old man. "You will see what happens."

Quickly the princess did as the old man told her. At once a great lake formed between the pursuing bear and the two humans it wanted to catch.

Although darkness came, the old man guided the princess safely to the house of her father in the Haida village. When she turned to thank her guide, he was no longer by her side, and the princess knew that she had been on the trail with a shaman of great power, perhaps a transformer, who had saved her from the bear.

*   *   *

Little-People Magic
Micmac

Many Indian tribes believed in dwarves, elves, and other tiny beings with fairy power: beings whom they sometimes called the Little People. These tiny beings were said to have magic powers. Because of this, they were to be treated kindly, or bad luck would follow. Midget Indians, they possessed all the Indian liking for merrymaking and jokes. This is why they were considered mischievous.

The tiny beings sometimes lived in little underground dwellings, but they also lived above ground, in little houses made of stones piled together. When a big human being moved these rocks or accidentally knocked them over, the Little People gathered the stones and put them back in place again. Indian children, who noticed the smallest things, were often puzzled by this. Sometimes they kept moving the stones, until warned by a grown-up that it was very unwise to do this, because misfortune might follow.

One morning, long, long ago, a Micmac maiden was bathing in a river. Suddenly she saw something which looked like a short branch, or a little pile of leaves, apparently carried along by the current. When it came nearer, she was astonished to see that the object was a tiny canoe, paddled by a little elf. She caught the canoe with great care in her hands, and took it to the skin lodge of her parents.

The parents were afraid. "This is a magic thing," they said, "and you should not have disturbed him. Carry him back carefully and put him exactly where you found him."

The little girl cried, because she did not want to lose what seemed to be a live doll. Before she could say anything, the tiny man spoke for the first time. "Do what your parents command!" he exclaimed in a high, piping voice.

Afraid, the girl ran back to where she had taken the canoe and its little paddler from the stream, and set it down carefully on the water. "My thanks," said the little man before he paddled away. "Some day I shall come back and see you again."

Then the little man paddled away, through rough water and over a little falls, guiding his frail canoe with great skill through the rapids.

The little girl thought the tiny man very nice. She feared for his safety and ran along the river bank, to rescue him if his canoe became swamped. She supposed that the little man knew why she followed him along the bank, for he looked back when he reached smooth water, and waved to her in a friendly way with his little paddle. She felt sure that the elf would keep his promise to come back; so every morning she went down to the stream to see if she could sight him, but she did not.

Some days later, she was gathering berries with some girl friends when, to her delight, she saw ten tiny canoes paddling downstream, keeping close to the bank where the girls were standing open-mouthed. They were astonished but not afraid, because the girl who had already met the tiny man had told them of her adventure. The leader in the first canoe waved his paddle and greeted his young friend with a cheery "Ho!"

The party of elves landed at the edge of the stream, where the girls stood. The chief of the little band, the elf whom the little girl had already met, went to one side and spoke with the other tiny men in a language which the girls did not understand. Whatever they said must have been very amusing, because they jumped about in glee, laughing and capering.

At first the chief did not seem to agree with whatever they were planning to do; but at last he smiled, pulled his long, white beard and, in the Micmac language, asked the little girl and her friends if they would like to go across to the other side of the river. "There are more berries there," he piped.

The girls laughed merrily, knowing that even all ten of the canoes put together could not carry one girl. At last, they agreed to cross the stream with the little people. At once the little men got their canoes and held them close to the bank by skillful paddling. "Step into my canoe," said the chief.

To please him, the little girl who had once carried him off, pretended to step into his tiny canoe. Much to her surprise, and that of the other girls, as soon as her foot touched the canoe, the craft became as big as a regular Micmac canoe and the little men grew as large as the Micmac Indians, while the girl seemed to become smaller.

The other girls did not wish to show themselves less brave than their companion, so each stepped into a canoe. By the same magic as that used by their chief, each canoe at once became as large as a regular canoe, while the man at the paddle became big enough to handle the canoe with ease. As happened to the first girl to board one of these canoes, each girl appeared to grow smaller.

Side by side, the paddlers seeming untroubled by the current, the canoes reached the other bank of the river, about a hundred yards away. Once the girls stepped on shore, they became their usual size. The paddlers raised their paddles in a salute, and the canoes shrank quickly to dwarf size. Then the canoes seemed to disappear in the direction of the rapids.

As the chief of the elves had said, there were many berries on the river bank where the girls had landed, and their baskets were soon full. Then the eldest girl in the band suddenly called out, "How are we going to get back to the other side of the river?"

✳ ✳ ✳

The Magic Seal
Squamish

Stanley Park, in the Vancouver of today, used to be the site of the chief village of the powerful Squamish people and their confederacy. From this central village, powerful canoes, carrying many armed war-

riors, set out on raids which led over ocean and inlets to the surrounding islands. This village was the home of famed chiefs and mighty medicine men, of whom none was more skilled in the art of medicine and magic than Ts'ak. He was a friend of the mighty chief Kapalana and had much power in the councils of the Squamish people.

A great raid by sea, planned by the Squamish to capture supplies and slaves, was led by the brother of Chief Kapalana. The attack was successful and the leader captured a beautiful Kwakiutl girl. Tribal law ruled that she, like all other captives, men and women, was to become a slave.

When the victorious Squamish returned to their village, the usual feasting and rejoicing took place. The people were surprised to find that the chief who led the raid and should have led the rejoicing showed little interest in the ceremonies. He was silent, grave, and thoughtful.

After a great feast, the captives were led before Chief Kapalana and his councilors. The great fire which lit the beautifully carved and painted ceremonial hall shone on many prisoners. Men, women, and children were taken one by one before the mighty chief. Their long hair was then cut short as a sign that they were now slaves of the Squamish.

When the beautiful Kwakiutl girl was brought before Chief Kapalana, something happened which had never before been seen in the memory of the oldest Squamish.

Chief Kapalana's brother strode to where the chief of all the Squamish sat. "Mighty chief, nobles and chiefs of the Squamish people, you have long told me that as a chief I should marry. For many moons I have thought of your wise words. Now I will abide by them. I wish this young woman, whom I took in battle with her powerful tribe, for my wife."

His words brought cries of wonder and many shouts of protest from the shocked gathering of nobles and people. They were angry that a chief, a prince of the Squamish, should defy tribal customs and choose a slave girl for his wife.

Chief Kapalana raised his hand for silence. "Though it has never been known before in the history of our people, what my brother asks may be a good thing. I give my brother the maid and wish them well."

No one dared question the decision of Chief Kapalana, and so a slave-girl became the wife of a warrior-chief.

Happy years followed for the chief and his bride. She helped him in all things and made him glad. It was only when their four sons grew to be young men that the hidden jealousy of the Squamish people was seen. The four sons were more skillful in sports and war than all of the other youths of the village.

"Why," the people asked in secret, "should the sons of a slave-woman be better hunters, fishermen, and warriors than the sons of free women?"

The bitterness of the people grew until one day Ts'ak, the medicine man, learned that the lives of the four young men were in danger. Moving silently in the forest one day, he overheard a number of young men of his tribe planning to ambush and kill the four sons of "the slave-woman."

"You must not do this thing," the shaman said as he stepped from his hiding place. "Their father is a brave chief who deserves well of his people. Squamish blood flows in the veins of the young men whom you plan to kill, and they are nephews of my friend, the great Chief Kapalana. My magic will find a way to rid the people of the young men who have put you all to shame by their skill. Do nothing until I command you. I have spoken."

The young men, who greatly feared the magic power of the shaman, agreed to await his orders.

As the sun flooded the west with a blood-red light, Ts'ak pulled his canoe up on the beach at Squamish. He went into the forest until he reached a little lake, an inlet of the ocean, circled by huge cedars. He chose the largest of the mighty trees which stood by the water's edge and with stone axe and fire he started the task of felling it. When the sun had left for the third time, the giant tree crashed to the ground. When the sun came again, it saw the medicine man cutting and carving the tree with his stone tools.

For three suns more, the shaman, aided by fire, shaped the huge cedar log until it no longer looked like a log. Now a mighty seal lay where the log had been. Ts'ak made a powerful medicine oil from strange herbs, fish oil, and the heads of snakes. He rubbed this oil on the head, flippers, and tail of the great seal. Then he prayed, sang, and danced in a circle around it. He shook his rattle alongside the seal's head. The animal moved! He sang again a power-medicine song and the seal stirred and slid into the water.

The shaman camped at the inlet for seven suns, training the great seal for its part in his scheme.

When Ts'ak returned to the village, he held a secret meeting in the forest with those who had planned to kill the sons of the slave-woman.

"Tomorrow, just as the tide begins to run out, a great seal will swim close to the shore, directly in front of our village. Watch for it. As soon as you see it, run for your harpoons and spears, shouting and pointing to the seal. Do not go out after it in your canoes, and tell the other young men of the village not to do so. Only the sons of the slave-woman must hunt the seal. I have spoken."

The medicine man spoke truly. Next day, at the turn of the tide, a huge seal leapt and played in the ocean in front of the village. The young men shouted and ran to their houses as though to get their weapons, but the four sons of the slave-woman were the first to arm themselves for the chase, and put off in their big canoe. Without waiting for the others, they paddled swiftly toward the seal. When they were within striking distance, the eldest brother stood up in the bow of the canoe and threw his harpoon. The sharp weapon sank deeply into the seal's shoulder. The head of the harpoon was fastened to the young man's wrist by a long, strong length of braided whale sinew. A moment later, one of the other brothers had also set his harpoon in the animal's side. It now began to swim strongly through the Narrows, out into the waters of the great gulf. To try to slow the speed of the seal, the two other brothers also drove their harpoons deep into its body.

When the canoe was being towed at a speed which meant death, far from land, the oldest son shouted to his brothers to cut the seal loose. He tried to cut the thong around his wrist, but the sharp stone knife did not even mark the sinew. Neither he nor his brothers could loosen the thongs from their wrists, and soon they knew that they were prisoners of a magic seal.

On and on they were towed toward the Valdez Islands. Just as the sun sank, the astonished brothers saw the great seal change into a cedar log. The harpoons fell into the ocean, and as the brothers were pulling them into the canoe, a sudden squall hit their craft. The young men seized their paddles, but a great wave caught up their canoe and carried it high onto the shore of a distant island. They liked the land and decided to live there.

When the brothers' skill as fishermen and hunters became known, they married daughters of chiefs of surrounding islands. Soon the young men became leaders in the councils of the island tribes.

*   *   *

Medicine Rock

Squamish

The Squamish sailed his heavily-laden canoe slowly through the calm waters of Burrard Inlet. Vancouver could be seen in the far distance and Point Grey stood out ahead. Then the slight breeze died.

"Shall I whistle for a wind, Tillicum?" asked the author.

"I shall be glad if you will," he answered.

I whistled three low, long notes that some seamen use successfully to conjure up a wind, often from a favorable direction. The charm, the secret of which I know not, had often worked for me and I hoped that it would not fail me now, since I did not want to lose face and disprove "white man's magic" before my Squamish friend.

I was not disappointed. In a few moments, a breeze rippled the calm water and soon the canoe was sailing toward Point Grey, with a "bone in her teeth."

As we rounded the southwest of the Point, my Indian friend lowered the sail and brought the canoe to a stop with a few strokes of his paddle. He pointed toward a big rock which loomed up in the dusk. "Homolsom," he said.

"Do you know the legend of this rock?" he asked. "It is the rock which Indians sailing these waters use instead of whistling for wind," he said.

"Tell me the legend, Tillicum," I said.

"This great rock was not always there," he began. "Once, long, long before the white men came, there was a powerful spirit, known to our people as the Tyee of the Wind of the West. He blew up such terrible storms that even the Great Spirit called on his Four Men of Magic and sent them on a mission to overcome the terrible Tyee of the Wind of the West. As the giant canoe carried The Four out through the troubled waters of the Pacific, the Tyee saw them coming.

" 'Now you shall feel my power,' he boasted. 'I will tear your canoe apart and you shall drown where the fish swim!' The Tyee then whistled up a wind. It grew until it became a great storm and then a terrible hurricane. Mountain-high waves lashed the shores of the strait, the channels, and the inlets. Islands were torn apart, and huge tree branches were driven through the dark skies like the feathers of eagles.

"All through this awful storm, the medicine-magic of their spirit canoe carried The Four through the terrible storm. Nearer and nearer they came to the dwelling place of the now frightened Tyee of the Wind of the West. He decided to make his last stand on the point of land known today as Point Grey.

"Swiftly the magic canoe beached itself on the end of the point. The Four Men of Magic, commanding the Tyee to still his winds and tempest, sprang ashore. The wind and storm faded into a great silence and the frightened and humbled Tyee stood silent on the end of the point.

" 'Evil one with heart of stone, you have defied the Great Spirit and brought death to many. Now you shall pay for your wicked deeds,' cried The Four. 'You shall continue to live, but as a rock, kept clean by the waters of the ocean. From now on and forever will you help, not hinder, our people who sail these waters.'

"Not one sound broke the silence as the Tyees continued, 'When there is no wind and canoes float motionless on the waters which surround you, you will blow up a fair wind so that they may sail again.'

"Then, slowly, the Tyee of the Wind of the West turned into this great rock, and from that time, as he had been commanded, he was the servant, not the master, of all who sailed these waters.

"See, he still stands," said my Squamish guide, pointing to the huge rock which rose up directly in front of us.

Stars gleamed in the blue-black sky. Night had fallen and with it the wind. Not a breath of breeze ruffled the dark waters. "Shall I take a paddle, Tillicum?" I asked.

The Squamish made no reply, but a stroke of his paddle brought the canoe almost alongside the Homolsom Rock. Softly he touched it with the blade of his paddle, then he backed water so that his canoe floated free of the rocky shore. He hoisted the sail and sat silently in the stern of the canoe for a few moments. I did not speak.

Suddenly I felt the touch of a light breeze on the back of my neck. The sail filled, and a breeze blew steadily until the Squamish beached his canoe at Vancouver.

* * *

The Magic Mud Things
Pawnee

The Pawnee storytellers often tell this tale, but it is told also by storytellers of other tribes of the Great Plains.

Long ago, the Indians had no ponies and hunted buffalo and travelled for many moons on foot. When they moved camp to follow the buffalo herds, the women of the tribes were aided by big, strong dogs. These dogs dragged the heavy tepees, and everything else that

had to be transported, on travois. At the story-fire, this is a story that was told by the storytellers.

In a big camp of the Pawnees dwelt a poor boy who was an orphan. In order to get food, he had to beg from tepee to tepee. Some of the people were good to him, and the chief most of all. He gave the boy food, moccasins, and sometimes leggings.

The chief told his people, "Tirawa, the Great Spirit, knows that this little boy lives. As the boy grows, Tirawa will certainly watch over him, and one day this boy may become a great chief."

The people laughed when they were alone, because they did not believe the words of the chief.

One night the boy had a vision-dream in which he saw two strange, big things, like great deer; but the animals of which he dreamed had long hair instead of antlers, and their tails were long and bushy. The boy did not know what sort of animals he had seen. He made small figures from mud, just like the things he had dreamed. He did not tell the people about them.

Soon another spirit-dream came to the boy in the night; and he was given a magic song, which he believed must come from Tirawa. The boy was also told that the things he had seen were animals which would need grass to eat and water to drink, as the deer did. So the boy put his two mud figures in a hidden valley where there was a little lake and much grass.

For many moons, the boy visited the things which he had made. Then, one night in a dream, a mysterious voice told him to go to the valley where he had hidden the mud creatures. "Take a long strip of rawhide with you," he was told.

The boy got the rawhide from the chief, who had become more and more friendly. Though the boy was afraid, he went to the valley and found that his two mud animals were now alive, beautiful, and friendly. Showing no fear, they came to the boy. He put the ends of the strips of rawhide around their beautiful necks and led them back to the village. The boy believed that the two spirit things, which were later known as ponies, came from the skies.

At first the people were afraid, and treated the strange new animals as things of magic. The boy led the animals to the chief, who later adopted the boy.

Soon the tribe discovered how wonderful and useful the two animals were.

As the chief had foretold, the boy became a great warrior when he became older, and he formed the great Society of the Chiefs, which accepted only the bravest and most skillful warrior-chiefs as members.

The First Blackfish

Tlingit

Natsihlane of the Tlingit was a good hunter. Because of this, his elder brother-in-law was very jealous of him. Natsihlane's younger brother-in-law was fond of him, and one day when the two brothers were about to leave on a hunt, the younger one asked that Natsihlane be taken along. This suited the plans of the older brother, because after a long journey by canoe to a far distant island, they went ashore to separate and hunt in different parts of it. When Natsihlane got back to where they had left the canoe, he saw his brothers-in-law paddling far from shore.

"Come back!" Natsihlane shouted, throwing a deer which he had killed and slung across his shoulders onto the beach. He saw the younger man in the canoe try to paddle back toward the island, but the elder brother proved too strong for him and the canoe disappeared into the distance. Natsihlane was sad and wondered how he would ever escape from the island, for he had no tools with which to make a dugout canoe. At last, he fell asleep by his fire on the shore and dreamed that he heard a strange voice say, "Awake. The one sent to get you is here."

He awakened but could see nothing. He thought that he had only heard a dream-voice, so he went to sleep again. The voice came again as he slept and again he started up. This time he saw a big gull and a half-grown sea lion on the beach not far from him. Natsihlane lay down again and pretended to sleep, but he kept good watch from under his blanket. He saw the gull come close to his blanket and heard it speak.

The Tlingit sprang up and exclaimed, "I heard you speak!"

"You did," the gull answered. "I said, the one sent to get you is here. Follow me."

They went to the edge of the ocean and he saw the sea lion in the water. It said, "I have come for you. The sea lion chief wishes to see you. Climb on my back but keep both eyes tightly closed until I tell you to open them again."

Natsihlane obeyed because he knew that there was strong medicine at work. After the sea lion had swum for a long time, Natsihlane felt it climb out of the water. "Open your eyes," it said. The Tlingit did so and found that he was on a great rock beside a cliff. The rock opened and the Tlingit found himself inside a great house. Though the people inside it looked like humans to him, he sensed that they must be sea lions.

The chief of the sea lions sat on a great carved chair. "When you have helped my son, we will help you in your trouble," he said.

The chief pointed behind him and Natsihlane saw a sea lion lying on the floor with a shaman shaking a rattle over him. The Tlingit, who could often work magic when he could call up the right spirit power, saw that there was a sharp bone harpoon point sticking in the sea lion's side, just beneath the skin.

"I will cure your son, if you will see that I reach my home on the mainland, O Chief," said the Tlingit.

"It shall be as you wish," declared the chief.

Natsihlane believed that the old chief spoke with a straight tongue and soon removed the harpoon point from the wounded sea lion.

The chief thanked the Tlingit, offered him rich foods, then ordered some slaves to fill the dried stomach of a sea lion with air. This they did, and put some food and fresh water inside. Before putting the Tlingit inside the stomach, the chief said, "Thoughts are powerful medicine when they are used well. Think hard of the beach beside your village. Do not let your thoughts stray off on other trails and be sure not to think of this house."

The slaves pushed the sea lion's stomach out into the ocean and it began to float rapidly away. Inside it, Natsihlane thought of the sea lion chief who had befriended him. Quick as a loon dives, he was back, bobbing up and down just outside the chief's house door.

Once again the slaves pushed him out into the ocean. This time he kept his thoughts fixed on the beach close to his house. Soon after, he was washed up on that beach. He split open the sea lion's stomach with his knife, left his strange craft, and hid himself in the forest.

He decided not to go home until he had thought of a way to be revenged on his evil brother-in-law. An inner voice spoke to him. He cut branches from different trees and began to carve. He made eight big fish from spruce branches and painted stripes on them with clay which he found nearby. He put them in a row on the beach, close to the ocean. He said some medicine words over them and then ordered them to jump into the water. They sprang into the ocean at his command, but lay lifeless on the surface. He then cut eight more fish from red cedar, laid them in a row on the sand, sang medicine songs to them and ordered them into the ocean. They entered the water, swam around a little, then were washed up by the incoming tide. He made fish from hemlock, but they would not live either.

"Once more will I try," he vowed. He worked by moonlight and carved eight fish from yellow cedar. He did his very best work and painted each fish with a white stripe across the head and a circle on the dorsal fin. Never before had he seen fish like them, but he placed them in line, as he had done the others, and danced and sang his most powerful spirit songs for them. Then, as the raven cawed a greeting to morning, he commanded the fish to leap into the water and swim and live. They did so, and soon the tide washed up foam from their spouting, because they had grown greatly and become black whales. They brought fish to Natsihlane and obeyed his orders.

When at last he saw his brother-in-law's canoe in the distance, he called the blackfish to him. "Swim out and destroy that canoe and see that all in it drown except the youngest. Bring him safely to me."

Swift as salmon, the eight fish raced toward the distant canoe. Soon Natsihlane saw them surround it and it disappeared. The Tlingit feared for a while for the safety of his younger brother-in-law, but soon saw him riding safely on the backs of two of the blackfish which swam side by side to Natsihlane. He called them out of the water and they formed a line on the shore again.

"I made you to get revenge," he told them. "That was a bad thing to do. You must never again harm any human being."

Having so told them, he let them go and they swam far out into the ocean and disappeared. They were the first blackfish to swim the seas.

* * *

Shamans' Magic

Salish

Long, long ago, a young Salish chief had a wife whom he loved very well. Deep in the red cedar forest, she told him one day when summer had come, "Today is the day when our child will be born."

The young chief was very glad. Then, as was the custom among their people, they both went swimming to purify themselves. Together they swam far. After a time, they left the water on the shore of what is now called Stanley Park. The young chief led his wife into the forest nearby, where she could be alone. She told him to come in the morning and find them both. When he left her, she heard the otter-like sound as he quietly entered the water again and continued to swim.

Fate played a part in the lives of these people, as it often seems to do today. The Segalie Tyee, the Great Spirit of the Indians of the Northwest Coast, had on that day sent his Four Men, messengers and makers of magic, on a mission. Their great canoe was approaching the lone swimmer. They saw the young chief and shouted to him to get out of their way at once. They knew that if one of their paddles or their canoe should touch a human being, either they would lose power or the human perish.

The young man refused to change his course and continued to swim directly in the path of the huge canoe. He would not get out of the way even for the Four Men, who were powerful shamans. Thinking of his son to be born, the young man felt that this day was his day and not even magic could harm him. He also wanted his son to know that the father was not afraid of anything.

The Four Men talked together. They were astonished and annoyed by the foolish action of the young chief. Still, they admired his great courage. They decided to honor him in a special way, so that he and his wife and child would live forever as a symbol of the power of the Segalie Tyee. This the Four Men did by turning the young man and his family into rocks, which have lasted even until this day. The rock, known as Siwash Rock, rises above the water on the west side of Stanley Park; and his wife and son are two rocks, a large one and a little one, the Indians believe, standing in the woods close by.

✳   ✳   ✳

Animal and Bird
Folktales

The Goat Guide

Tsimshian

On the jagged mountain peaks of the River of the Mists, many families of mountain goats made their homes. In the valleys, at the foot of the mountains, lived a tribe of Tsimshian Indians. Both the Indians and the goats lived carefree lives. There was plenty of food and all was well, until the Indians disobeyed the commands of the Sky Chief, who had told his children to hunt and fish only when they needed food. Never were they to kill his creatures without good reason.

After a time, the Indians disobeyed the law and began hunting the mountain goats of the high peaks for sport. The hunters knew how the goats nearly always looked down from the high places in search of enemies. Taking advantage of this, the Indians shot downward from the highest peaks and killed and wounded many goats on the lower crags. The hunters did not need meat, so the wounded animals were left to die. When the goats learned to look up as well as down for their cruel foes, the Indians trained dogs to hunt the goats with them. Through high mountain passes, the dogs drove the goats, worrying them and often driving them over high cliffs to their death on the rocks beneath.

A young chief of the tribe, who obeyed the wishes of the Sky Chief and only hunted when he needed food, liked to climb high in the mountains. He ascended the highest peaks for the pleasure of watching the goat clans play and leap from crag to crag. The animals had learned not to fear Raven Feather, for that was the name of the young chief. They seemed to know that he had no harm for them in his heart, but all this had been forgotten since the Indian hunters cruelly killed the goats without reason.

One day, when Raven Feather climbed among the high peaks, he saw many dead goats lying in the gorges and his heart was heavy. In a cave he found a young mountain goat bleating sadly beside its dead mother. She had three arrows in her back and her fine white coat was stained scarlet with her blood. The young chief took the baby goat in his arms, and at the risk of falling from the high and slippery ledges, carried it safely back to the village.

The older people mocked Raven Feather and called him "goat chief," but he did not care what they said, for his inner voice told him that he had done what was right in the eyes of the Sky Chief. The young goat was well-fed and cared for by Raven Feather and it followed him about like a dog. Often the dogs of the village tried to attack the goat, but the young chief drove them off with blows from a heavy stick, and soon they bothered the pet goat no more.

One day, two strangers came to the Indian village. Though the people of the village did not know from which tribe their visitors came, they gave their guests food and shelter because they wore rich robes and looked and acted like chiefs and shamans. The village dogs growled fiercely and threatened the two visitors, but slunk off with terrified yelps when the strangers looked hard at them. The visitors remained for two suns and when they left they invited all of the Indians in the village to a great potlatch and mask dance in their village high in the mountains. Even the old men of the tribe did not seem to know where the village of the strangers was, but they were all so eager to go to the potlatch, in the hope of rich presents, that one of the strangers decided to stay until the sun came again and act as guide. The other visitor left to tell his chief and people that their visitors from the valley would arrive before the sun left next day.

When the tribe set out next morning, Raven Feather took his goat with him. It was half-grown now and never left the young chief's side. The people laughed and sneered at the idea of taking a goat to a potlatch. "Those who invited us will think that you are not a chief but a goat mother," they mocked. The young chief only smiled.

"That you may do," said the stranger-guide when the hunters, seeing Raven Feather's goat go along, asked if they could take their dogs along.

The hunters had hoped to hunt goats on the way to their guide's village, but though they traveled up into the high places from the time the sun came until it hung low over the mountain peaks of the west, they saw not one goat. The tribe arrived at a village of fine houses in a valley high in the mountains. Two great community houses were decorated and ready for the feast, and the best foods were piled high inside. After the village chief and shaman had greeted them, the visitors sat down to feast. They were surprised that Raven Feather was invited to sit next to the village chief on the opposite side of the house from the rest of his tribe. The goat, which seemed to feel at home, sat next to him.

After feasting for some time, the village chief said, "We leave you now to make ready for a mask dance; our people are glad that you are here."

As the visitors continued to feast, they saw people wearing mountain goat masks and skin robes looking in at the doorways. "The dancers are getting ready," they thought. Only their hunting dogs were uneasy. They lay shivering at the feet of their owners, whining softly and refusing to eat the scraps tossed to them. After a while, the village chief and the dancers returned. They were dressed as goats and were so like them in appearance that they skipped and spun in the masked dance like real goats. One huge dancer with big feet jumped high in the air. "Wait till I kick the mountain side!" he shouted. "Just wait!"

The dogs whined loudly and an old visiting chief sprang to his feet. "There is bad medicine here," he said. As he spoke, the big dancer leaped over the fire, then sprang over the heads of the visitors, landing outside of the house. He kicked the mountain side and there was a loud rumbling. The houses quivered and shook. Then the mountain seemed to fall apart. The walls of the houses disappeared and the frightened visitors saw that they were no longer in a high valley. They were sitting on the edge of a high precipice which began to fall away in a great rockslide.

The pet goat tugged at the ceremonial robe which Raven Feather wore. He saw that he could do nothing to help his people because a great chasm had opened up between them and where he stood. He followed his goat, and swiftly and surely it led him through a narrow, winding, hidden gorge, down the mountain side to safety.

All of the rest of his tribe and their dogs were killed. The goat people were revenged.

Today, great talking sticks of cedar, the totem poles of the young chief and his descendants, have a mountain goat carved in the place of honor, for Raven Feather adopted the mountain goat as his family crest.

✳   ✳   ✳

White Egg, Blue Egg
Pueblo

Before creation began, there was no one on the land. When the Pueblo people were created, they found their world dark and they saw nothing. When at last light came, they were afraid of what they saw; and it

was a long time before they got used to the strange place in which
they lived. But this was soon to change. When the people saw how
strange they looked, they made coverings for their bodies out of leaves
and grass, and made foot coverings to protect their feet from the stony
ground. It was not long before the people wanted nicer things, and
more things than their neighbors.

The Sky Father and Earth Mother saw this and were sad. They
sent Yanauluha, a great and wise medicine man, to help and work
among the people. He brought them water and plants, and many
things which gave the people comfort. Among his magic things was a
beautiful medicine staff of many bright colors. It was covered with
ornaments, shells, feathers of all colors, and precious things which
sparkled when the staff was moved. The shells not only decorated the
staff, but they also made a loud sound like bells, when the staff was
held above the head of the medicine man. When the people heard the
sound, they gathered to see what their leader wanted.

One sunny day, the people had gathered to hear the medicine
man speak. But he was silent as he held his staff in his right hand, and
struck it sharply with his left hand.

By his magic, two white and two blue eggs appeared at once. The
people were told that the eggs were the seeds of living things, which
would help to make the world more fruitful. Then there was a wild
rush for the eggs. They did not break, because they were eggs of great
magic; but the people who wanted most fought hardest for the eggs,
and were able to seize the two blue eggs before the others had a
chance. The others had to be content with the two white eggs.

When the big day came that the two blue eggs hatched, little dark-
colored birds with rough skins came out of the eggshells. The chicks
looked as though they might grow beautiful as they became older. The
white eggs showed no signs of hatching, so the people watched the
chicks from the blue eggs grow and fed them much food. The chicks
were very greedy and fought to see which could eat the most. When
the feathers came, they were jet black and glossy, and the people saw
that the birds were ravens. Soon the birds flew away with harsh,
mocking cries at the people who had expected so much.

Then, one sunny day, the white eggs broke open and at once
brightly colored macaws hopped out. As these birds winged their way
southward, the people were glad because they knew that birds of great
beauty would soon brighten their world, and the feathers of these
birds would decorate the tribal prayer sticks.

✳   ✳   ✳

The Tired Wolf

Tlingit

One day, when men of the Wolf Clan of the Tlingit were out fishing, far from shore, they saw a dark shadow moving slowly in the water, some distance away from them. They paddled quickly toward it, and found a wolf swimming so slowly that it hardly moved in the water. Its eyes were nearly closed, and the poor beast was so tired that its tongue hung out. The animal could hardly keep its head above water. Friendly hands pulled it into the canoe, and the Tlingit took the wolf to their village.

For many years, the wolf lived with them. It always hunted with the men who had saved its life. Because it could always follow trails to where deer and other animals could be found, the clan never lacked meat. The wolf lived with its rescuers for so long that the people began to think of it as a member of the clan.

One day, the old wolf lay on a mat in front of the house of the clan chief. Its friends gathered sadly around it, for they knew that it was very old and about to take the Shadow Trail. Just as the sun sank, the wolf died. The next night, a man of the clan heard its relatives singing a death song for it. Their voices rose and fell in a wailing dirge which filled the forest with sadness.

From then on, the song was used by the clan as a mourning song, and a figure of the tired wolf was carved and painted on their houseposts.

* * *

Dogs of the Sea Wolf
Haida

Wasko, the great sea wolf, hunter of whales of the Haida Islands, was hunted only by the most daring hunters among the Haida. Others never even tried to trap these huge dogs because they were so fierce and strong. One brave hunter, who had tried to trap these giant beasts with beams and nets and sliding nooses, was not successful. But he was favored by his helpful spirits, so that he was fortunate enough to find two of these sea wolves while on the hunting trail.

The hunter lived with his wife at Hunter's Point. When he tramped through the cedar forest each day on his way to Skidegate, the home of the parents of his wife, he thought sometimes that he heard strange, loud whining as he returned to the Point. Each day, he looked in different parts of the trail to see if he could find out what was making the strange noises, but never could he find the spirit beasts which called. Then one day he looked into the hollow of a huge, dead cedar tree and found two great half-starved creatures that looked like very strange dog puppies. He managed to drag them one at a time to his house, where he and his wife raised them. Quickly they grew into huge, dog-like creatures; and the hunter knew that they were Waskos, mysterious wolf dogs of the sea. The beasts were savage, as were all of their kind, but they seemed to know that their lives had been saved by the hunter, and they seemed to like these two humans who fed them huge meals each day.

Early one morning, the hunter saw his wolf dogs far out at sea, surrounded by whales; and soon the dogs swam ashore, bringing with

them six whales which they had killed. From then on, the Waskos
hunted whales every night and sometimes by daylight, and brought
back more whales than the hunter and all of his clan needed for food.
The hunter and his people smoked the whale meat and fat, and stored
the precious fat in great cedar chests. He also shared the catches of his
hunting dogs with the parents of his wife at Skidegate. One day the
hunter and his wife were stormbound at Skidegate for a long time,
until they had eaten all of the food stored in the home of her parents.
When he was hungry, the hunter told his wife to ask her mother to
share some dried salmon eggs, which she had hidden away in the
stomach of a whale. But the mother-in-law was a miser and would not
part with any of the eggs.

When the savage storm passed and the ocean was smooth again,
the hunter, his wife, and his mother-in-law paddled his canoe back to
Hunter's Point. The mother was astonished and jealous when she saw
the two great Waskos, surrounded by many whales which the dogs
had caught and dragged onto the beach, in front of the house of their
master. Now the mother-in-law told her daughter to split open the
stomach of the whale and share the salmon eggs with her husband.
The hunter refused, saying that it was too late to offer food now when
they had plenty once again.

To punish his mother-in-law for being a miser, the hunter poured
rotten whale grease on mussels, clams, and other seafood on the beach,
knowing that the woman was very fond of them. Then, bad trouble
came between the mother and the hunter. For revenge, she arose very
early one morning, made a magic potion, put hot stones in it, and
poured the mixture into the sea. This caused a severe storm, so that
nobody dared leave their houses for some days. The hunter was
greatly troubled about his valuable sea dogs which had been caught
far out at sea by the storm. He walked along the beach in the hope of
seeing them out in the ocean.

The hunter walked many miles, and when he could not see his
dogs, he climbed a mountain near his house to get a better view. He
strained his eyes for a long time, and then he saw them far out at sea,
swimming very slowly toward the shore. "They are too tired to reach
shore," the hunter thought, "and they will drown." But the sea dogs
fought their way closer and closer to shore. They tried to climb onto
land, but the place where they tried to go ashore was covered with
huge, slippery rocks, and a steep cliff rose behind them.

Unable to land, the two poor beasts, so tired that they hardly
seemed to move, headed for Skidegate Channel. "Now they are safe,"
thought the hunter, and he was glad. But he was glad too soon. The

Waskos dragged themselves onto the beach, where a point stuck out into the sea, and then changed into two huge rocks which can be seen today on the shore.

✳ ✳ ✳

Song of the Frog
Tlingit

A Tlingit Indian and his wife were paddling a fishing canoe across a wide lake. Swiftly a heavy fog covered the water. It was so thick that the Indians could not see each other. The wind died. They were lost. They paddled first in one direction, then in another, until they were almost too tired to hold a paddle. Nothing could they see. Suddenly, in the distance, they heard the sound of singing. The notes were high and shrill.

With new strength, they took up their paddles and set off in the direction of the mysterious singing. After a long time, they reached the place from which the sound seemed to come. They leaned far over the side of the canoe and saw that the singing sound was made by a little frog. It swam away, but they followed in the direction of the sound of its singing. For a long time they paddled after the frog. When they became too tired to paddle, the frog waited for them. All through the fog and darkness, they followed the sound trail of the song of the frog. When daylight came, the fog lifted and they were glad to see the shore in the far distance.

"This frog will I keep for mine," said the husband, as the canoe came up to it.

"It shall not be so," said the woman. "I want the frog to be mine."

For a long time they spoke of who should have the frog. At last the man told his wife that she could have it. Gently she picked it out of the water and put it on a blanket beside her. They reached shore safely and the woman tenderly carried the frog into the forest. She left it on the shore of a lovely little lake.

When the woman reached the village, she sang the song of the frog, which she had learned during the long voyage. The people listened and were pleased. Since that time, her people were known as the frog people and the song and the crest of the frog became theirs.

✳ ✳ ✳

Hunter of Eagles
Woodland

"Never do as the Hunter of Eagles did in the long past," warned the eastern Woodland story teller, as he began this tale.

The animals and birds are the friends of the Woodland people, so their hunters should never be cruel to them nor kill more than they need for food. Hunter of Eagles did, until he learned in a dream that his totem spirits did not like his treatment of the wild things.

This is what he used to do. From his grandfather he had received the gift of being able to call the beasts and birds to his hiding place, so that he could use his bow and arrows to shoot them easily. This, the hunters of the tribes and the people said, was a very bad thing to do, unless in time of bad famine. They warned him that the Great Spirit would surely punish him for these bad deeds, unless he changed his way of life.

He did not heed these warnings, and he would still call the eagles down from high in the sky by promises of much meat to take back to their eyries, where they nested and sometimes had baby eaglets. To kill eagles at these times was very bad, but Hunter of Eagles still tempted them down from the sky and shot them for their splendid feathers.

Then one day the huge mother of eagles swooped down from the skies to protect the baby birds of all eagle mothers. Hunter of Eagles saw her coming and had just enough time to creep inside a hollow log, when he heard the beating of the great eagle wings just outside. The great eagle seized the big log in her strong talons and flew away with it to her eyrie. Even though she flew very fast, many hornets and ants and other biting things inside the log tortured the hunter by stinging him all over his body. The mother of eagles dropped the log on the big ledge where her nest was, then flew off to hunt food for her three young. The hunter quickly wriggled out of the log and saw that he could not possibly escape from the high ledge. He had to think quickly of how he was going to escape death from the talons and savage beak of the eagle mother.

His strong bow and arrows had been left behind, but he still had his thin, strong leather carrying thongs, which he used to carry small animals and birds that he shot. Quickly he undid the thongs and tied one around the beak of each eaglet. Soon the mother bird returned carrying a rabbit. When she saw what the hunter had done, she was going to kill him, but first she tried to remove the thongs from the beaks of her babies. That she could not do, though she tried hard and long with both beak and talons. Night came and went twice, while she struggled to release her children, but she could not do so.

Then she was glad that she had not killed the hunter when she arrived back at her nest, because she hoped to make him release the thongs. Through his magic power, she was able to talk with him. She promised not to tear him to pieces if he would vow to do three things: first, to unfasten the thongs from the beaks of her babies; second, never to kill more deer than was needed for food; and third, the most important vow of all, never to kill an eagle without first getting permission from his totem spirits.

When he promised these things, the eagle mother told him that she would carry him back unharmed to where she had found him. Nearly starving, and with wonder filling his mind about the goodness of the great bird, he solemnly agreed to do everything that she had asked. After feeding her babies on the food which she had brought to the nest, she took Hunter of Eagles gently up in her huge talons, and flying swiftly down to earth, laid him almost on the same spot from which she had flown away with the log.

The hunter kept his three promises and both the deer and the eagles were glad. Hunter of Eagles had changed so much because of his adventure with the mother of eagles that he begged all of the hunters of his tribe to spare all deer and eagles whenever they could, and even to feed them when the winds of winter blew and snow covered the ground like a great white blanket. His descendants too kept his promises alive, and even when food was scarce and the tribe had hardly enough for the people, the family of Hunter of Eagles always called the deer and eagles to eat of the food which they had laid out for these beasts and birds.

✻ ✻ ✻

Trickster Trails

Tlingit

The Tlingit tell that Beaver and Porcupine were friends, when the world was young. Porcupine protected his companion from bears, and was patient when Beaver tricked him at times. The prickly one was not very clever and some of the animals made fun of him, but they took care to keep out of reach of his fast-striking tail when they did so. One day Beaver played a mean trick on his friend. He asked Porcupine to his lodge for a feast, though he knew that Porcupine could not dive under water to get into the lodge. Porcupine did not know this.

Beaver told Porcupine to climb onto his back and they started out for the lodge. When they got there, Beaver told his friend to follow

him and then dived down to the underwater door. Porcupine could not follow, so he climbed onto the roof of the lodge and waited for a long time for Beaver to come to the surface. When Beaver did not do so, and it began to grow dark, poor Porcupine dropped into the water and tried to swim to shore. His light quills kept him afloat, but he could not make any progress toward shore. He climbed back onto the top of the lodge and called loudly to his friend Wolverine to grant him the breath of the north wind. When Porcupine got this cold power, he froze the lake solid. Dropping onto the ice, Porcupine crawled slowly over the slippery surface to shore. He was very glad to reach his den, under a great rock, alive and was very angry at Beaver.

A few suns had come and gone before Porcupine saw Beaver again. Beaver was sitting at the edge of the lake, and he pretended to be angry because Porcupine had not followed him down to the feast. Porcupine said that he was sorry too and asked Beaver to visit the treetop trails with him. Beaver could hardly climb at all, but he thought that it would be nice to look down on the lake from the trees, and said that he would go if his friend would help him. Porcupine did help him toward the treetops, by using trails of half-fallen trees which sloped upward and along big cedar branches where Beaver felt safe. At last Porcupine got Beaver up onto the top branches of a tall tree. He left him there. Darkness had come and gone for the second time before Squirrel heard his cries for help. Beaver wanted to try to go down the tree tail first, but Squirrel showed him that it was better to climb down head first. Bushy Tail showed Beaver where to cut steps with his sharp teeth, and after a long time he reached the ground. From that time on, Beaver and Porcupine were no longer friends.

* * *

Fast As a Frog
Northwest Coast

A trickster frog of the Northwest Coast was loudly boasting to some of his frog friends of his speed. "Even a deer who dared to race with me would be left far behind," he declared.

A loud laugh came from the edge of a clearing, close to where the frogs sat. They looked and saw a big buck.

"Why do you laugh, Deer?" asked the boastful frog.

"Because your long tongue travels so much faster than your long legs, Frog," replied the deer.

"Then you fear not to race me?" asked Frog.

"No," answered Deer when he could stop laughing.

So a race between Frog and Deer was decided on. It was to be run when the sun rose next day. The race was to be a long one, through valleys and along the borders of marshes and streams, to a big boulder at the foot of a high hill. When darkness came, the loud croaking of assembled frogs could be heard everywhere.

Next day, when the sun came, many frogs had gathered at the place where the race was to begin. No deer had come to see the start of the race, because Deer had been ashamed to tell his friends that he was going to race a frog.

When a frog chief gave the "Go!" signal, Deer bounded away so fast that he did not see Frog start. Deer ran much slower after his first few great leaps, thinking how foolish he was to race with Frog. He changed his mind when he saw Frog hopping fast along the trail, not far in front of him. Deer ran faster and thought that he had left Frog far behind. Then he saw Frog leaping along in front of him again.

Deer now ran as fast as he could, but from time to time as he followed the trail along the edge of marshes and banks of streams, he saw Frog hopping along in front of him. Once Frog turned and waved to Deer, as if to say, "Hurry!" This made Deer very angry.

When most of the distance had been run, Deer bounded ahead of Frog and no longer saw him. Then he felt sure that he had passed Frog for the last time. Deer was right. He did not pass Frog again. When Deer reached the big red boulder, Frog was waiting for him at the foot of it. "You must have run slowly, Deer," he laughed.

Deer was so ashamed that he made no reply. He walked off into the forest with his head held low.

What Deer knew not was that the frog he had passed on the trail was not Frog, nor even one frog. Many frogs had helped cunning Frog win the race by hopping part way, joining in the race from different parts of the trail. As soon as the race had begun, Frog had started out for the red boulder. He went by a short and easy trail, so that he was waiting for Deer long before that tricked animal arrived.

※　※　※

Mink and the Salmon
Bella Coola

Mink was a clever, cunning animal, feared and respected by the other woodland wild things. One warm afternoon, he was sunning himself on a point of land in Bella Coola territory which was washed on both sides by the ocean. A distant salmon leapt high in air.

"Ho, Tillicum!" Mink called. "It is dangerous out there. Sea Otter may catch you. If I were you, I would play closer to the shore."

Because Mink had called the salmon "friend," it foolishly believed
him. The silvery fish took great leaps out of the water, coming closer
and closer to shore.

Mink smiled hungrily, and with false words of praise lured the big
fish nearer and nearer to the point. At last, after a great leap almost
twice as high as a man, the salmon landed on the rocky point. Mink
seized it while it lay stunned by the fall, and dragged it farther away
from the water. He looked greedily at the beautiful fish and began to
sing a feast song. Mink touched every part of the shining salmon with
a stick held between his sharp teeth and sang again. "Who will eat that
bit, I wonder? Who will eat this bit, I wonder?"

Because Mink sang the answers as well as the questions, the reply
was always the same, "Mink will eat the bit."

Two little Bella Coola boys heard Mink sing the feast song and
they went to him. "We are hungry," they said. "Please give us a part of
your great fish."

"No," replied Mink. "I will eat it all by myself."

The two boys went sadly into the forest. Then the older boy said,
"Let us hide and watch Mink. Maybe he will not be able to eat every
bite of so big a fish." As they lay silently watching, Mink became
sleepy from the warm rays of the sun. He rolled over onto his side and
slept.

Noiselessly the two boys crept up to where Mink lay. They picked
up the dead salmon and carried it into the forest.

"Mink must be punished because he would not share his food
with hungry ones," the elder boy said. He cut a piece from the salmon's head and went softly back to where Mink lay. Mink's mouth
was wide open and he snored loudly. The boy gently rubbed the piece
of salmon over Mink's teeth. Then he stole away with his friend to
feast in the forest.

The sun was leaving to make place for night when Mink awoke.
"Now to eat that salmon," he said to himself as he got up. Mink looked

everywhere for the fish but could not find it. He ran his tongue hungrily over his teeth and felt little pieces of salmon on them.

"I must have eaten that salmon while I slept," he told himself.

"No, I cannot have eaten it," he said, as his stomach told him how empty it was.

"But I must have eaten it," he cried, as once again he felt the taste of salmon in his mouth.

"No, the king salmon must have made magic while I slept and taken the salmon back to the ocean," he decided.

Mink slunk stealthily into the forest, urged on by a hunger which told him that wherever the salmon was, it was not inside him. He would have to hunt for his supper.

* * *

Prince of the Wolves

Tsimshian

The long, pitiful howl of a timber wolf came from the forest behind a Tsimshian village. The people were afraid and hungry. The winter food supply was almost gone and there was little left to eat. They thought perhaps the wolves were hungry too, hungry enough to attack the village, maybe. They listened fearfully, but heard only the loud, pitiful wail of one wolf.

A young chief, who was unafraid, said that he would go to the forest and see why the wolf howled. He took his bow and arrows and went. He worked his way through the thick undergrowth, toward the place where the wolf wailed. Soon he saw it in a little clearing in front of him. As he went toward the wolf, it opened its mouth in a snarl. Its ears lay flat on its head. The young chief knew this danger signal but he showed no fear.

He knelt down and held out a hand toward the wary wolf. The snarl stopped and once again a mournful howl filled the forest. The beast came nearer and nearer until it was within reach of the young chief. The howl died in its throat and a low whine came from its open mouth.

Seeming to lose fear, the beast went up to the kneeling chief and put its huge head on his knee. The young hunter looked into its mouth and his keen eyes saw blood flowing from a wound at the back of the beast's throat. Slowly the chief put his hand into the open mouth. His fingers reached into the throat and felt inside. There was a big splinter of bone stuck deep in the flesh. The wolf whined piteously as the chief worked the bone loose, until he was at last able to pull it out. It was a splintered bone from a deer.

As soon as the bone had been taken out, the wolf jumped around the chief and licked his hands. Then the beast gave a low, long howl. There were stealthy movements in the forest and the chief saw that he was ringed by a pack of eight timber wolves. He patted the wolf beside him on the head and it loped off into the forest at the head of the waiting pack.

When two suns had passed, the young chief heard the loud howls of a wolf at the edge of the forest. "It is the voice of the leader," he told himself as he went toward the sound.

When he reached the outer fringe of great cedars, he found that he was right. The wolf leader came to the chief at once, rubbed its great shaggy head against him and asked him, as a dog would have done, to follow deeper into the forest. The chief did so and found the wolf pack standing beside a deer which had just been killed. The wolves melted into the dusk of the forest. The chief was surprised and glad when the pack left the deer. He carried the buck back to the hungry people of his village.

Every day, as the sun was low in the sky and the shadowy fingers of night stretched toward the forest, the grateful wolf called to the chief. Always there was one or two deer ready for him to carry back to the village. Soon the chief and the wolf leader became good friends and they hunted together. They learned to understand each other's ways and hunting was always good when the prince hunted with his friend, the wolf. No longer was there hunger among his happy people.

The chief, who was a prince of his tribe, decided to give a great potlatch at which he might be given a new name which he had chosen. Famine still haunted the land. The best hunters found but little game. With the help of his wolf friends, the young prince was able to get much meat ready for the potlatch. He asked the wolf pack leader to have his pack hunt not only deer, but also marten, mink, and otter, so that he might have their valuable skins to give as presents to the chiefs and high-ranking guests who would come to his potlatch.

At the potlatch there was great feasting and gift giving. After three suns of ceremony, the old chief who directed the potlatch struck the floor sharply with his speaker's staff. There was silence in the great house. Then the young prince told the people that he would take the title and crest of Prince of the Wolves. The chiefs and people were glad. They thanked the young chief for his great help to the village in time of need.

To honor the meeting with the wolf and the taking of the name, Prince of the Wolves had a totem pole carved and painted. On top of the great pole a timber wolf with its mouth wide open looked down on the houses of the prince and his grateful people.

❋   ❋   ❋

How and Why Tales

How Fire Came to the Six Nations

Iroquois

Often, around the fire in the long house of the Iroquois, during the Moon of the Long Nights, this tale is told.

Three Arrows was a boy of the Mohawk tribe. Although he had not yet seen fourteen winters he was already known among the Iroquois for his skill and daring. His arrows sped true to their mark. His name was given him when with three bone-tipped arrows he brought down three flying wild geese from the same flock. He could travel in the forest as softly as the south wind and he was a skillful hunter, but he never killed a bird or animal unless his clan needed food. He was well-versed in woodcraft, fleet of foot, and a clever wrestler. His people said, "Soon he will be a chief like his father." The sun shone strong in the heart of Three Arrows, because soon he would have to meet the test of strength and endurance through which the boys of his clan attained manhood. He had no fear of the outcome of the dream fast which he was so soon to take. His father was a great chief and a good man, and the boy's life had been patterned after that of his father.

When the grass was knee-high, Three Arrows left his village with his father. They climbed to a sacred place in the mountains. They found a narrow cave at the back of a little plateau. Here Three Arrows decided to live for his few days of prayer and vigil. He was not permitted to eat anything during the days and nights of his dream fast. He had no weapons, and his only clothing was a breechclout and moccasins. His father left the boy with the promise that he would visit him each day that the ceremony lasted, at dawn.

Three Arrows prayed to the Great Spirit. He begged that soon his clan spirit would appear in a dream and tell him what his guardian animal or bird was to be. When he knew this, he would adopt that bird or animal as his special guardian for the rest of his life. When the dream came he would be free to return to his people, his dream fast successfully achieved.

For five suns Three Arrows spent his days and nights on the rocky plateau, only climbing down to a little spring for water after each sunset. His heart was filled with a dark cloud because that morning his father had sadly warned him that the next day, the sixth sun, he must return to his village even if no dream had come to him in the night. This meant returning to his people in disgrace without the chance of taking another dream fast.

That night Three Arrows, weak from hunger and weary from ceaseless watch, cried out to the Great Mystery. "O Great Spirit, have pity on him who stands humbly before Thee. Let his clan spirit or a sign from beyond the thunderbird come to him before tomorrow's sunrise, if it be Thy will." As he prayed, the wind suddenly veered from east to north. This cheered Three Arrows because the wind was now the wind of the great bear, and the bear was the totem of his clan. When he entered the cavern he smelled for the first time the unmistakable odor of a bear: this was strong medicine. He crouched at the opening of the cave, too excited to lie down although his tired body craved rest. As he gazed out into the night he heard the rumble of thunder, saw the lightning flash, and felt the fierce breath of the wind from the north. Suddenly a vision came to him, and a gigantic bear stood beside him in the cave. Then Three Arrows heard it say, "Listen well, Mohawk. Your clan spirit has heard your prayer. Tonight you will learn a great mystery which will bring help and gladness to all your people." A terrible clash of thunder brought the dazed boy to his feet as the bear disappeared. He looked from the cave just as a streak of lightning flashed across the sky in the form of a blazing arrow. Was this the sign from the thunderbird?

Suddenly the air was filled with a fearful sound. A shrill shrieking came from the ledge just above the cave. It sounded as though mountain lions fought in the storm; yet Three Arrows felt no fear as he climbed toward the ledge. As his keen eyes grew accustomed to the dim light he saw that the force of the wind was causing two young balsam trees to rub violently against each other. The strange noise was caused by friction, and as he listened and watched fear filled his heart, for, from where the two trees rubbed together a flash of lightning showed smoke. Fascinated, he watched until flickers of flame followed the smoke. He had never seen fire of any kind at close range nor had any of his people. He scrambled down to the cave and covered his eyes in dread of this strange magic. Then he smelt bear again and he thought of his vision, his clan spirit, the bear, and its message. This was the mystery which he was to reveal to his people. The blazing arrow in the sky was to be his totem, and his new name—Blazing Arrow.

At daybreak, Blazing Arrow climbed onto the ledge and broke two dried sticks from what remained of one of the balsams. He rubbed them violently together, but nothing happened. "The magic is too powerful for me," he thought. Then a picture of his clan and village formed in his mind, and he patiently rubbed the hot sticks together again. His will power took the place of his tired muscles. Soon a little wisp of smoke greeted his renewed efforts, then came a bright spark on one of the sticks. Blazing Arrow waved it as he had seen the fiery arrow wave in the night sky. A resinous blister on the stick glowed, then flamed—fire had come to the Six Nations!

✳ ✳ ✳

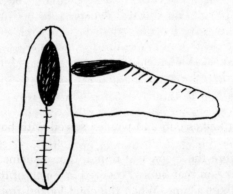

The First Moccasins

Plains

There was once a great chief of the Plains who had very tender feet. Other mighty chiefs laughed at him; little chiefs only smiled as he hobbled past; and though they did not dare to smile, the people of the tribe also enjoyed the big chief's discomfort. All of them were in the same canoe, having no horses and only bare feet, but luckily very few of them had tender feet. The unhappy medicine man who was advisor to the Chief-of-the-Tender-Feet was afraid and troubled. Each time he was called before the chief he was asked, "What are you going to do about it?" The "it" meant the chief's tender feet.

Forced by fear, the medicine man at last hit upon a plan. Though he knew that it was not the real answer to the chief's foot problem, nevertheless it was a good makeshift. The medicine man had some women of the tribe weave a long, narrow mat of reeds, and when the big chief had to go anywhere, four braves unrolled the mat in front of him so that he walked in comfort. One day, the braves were worn out from seeing that the chief's feet were not worn out. They carelessly unrolled the mat over a place where flint arrowheads had been chipped. The arrowheads had long ago taken flight, but the needle-sharp chips remained. When the big chief's tender feet were wounded by these chips, he uttered a series of whoops which made the nearby aspen tree leaves quiver so hard that they have been trembling ever since.

That night the poor medicine man was given an impossible task by the angry chief: "Cover the whole earth with mats so thick that my feet will not suffer. If you fail, you will die when the moon is round."

The frightened maker of magic crept back to his lodge. He did not wish to be put to death on the night of the full moon, but he could think of no way to avoid it. Suddenly he saw the hide of an elk which he had killed pegged to the ground, with two women busily scraping the hair from the hide, and an idea flashed into his groping mind. He sent out many hunters; many women were busy for many days; many braves with hunting knives cut, and women sewed with bone needles and rawhide sinews.

On the day before the moon was round, the medicine man went to the chief and told him that he had covered as much of the earth as was possible in so short a time. When the chief looked from the door of his lodge, he saw many paths of skin stretching as far as he could see. Long strips which could be moved from place to place connected the main leather paths. Even the chief thought that this time the magic of the medicine man had solved tenderfoot transportation for all time—but this was not to be!

One day, as the big chief was walking along one of his smooth, tough leather paths, he saw a pretty maiden of the tribe gliding ahead of him, walking on the hard earth on one side of the chief's pathway. She glanced back when she heard the pitter-patter of his feet on the elkhide pathway and seemed to smile. The chief set off on the run to catch up with her, his eyes fixed on the back of She-Who-Smiled, and so his feet strayed from the narrow path and landed in a bunch of needle-sharp thorns! The girl ran for her life when she heard the hideous howls of the chief, and Indians in the distant village thought that they were being attacked by wildcats.

Two suns later, when the chief was calm enough to speak again, he had his medicine man brought before him and told the unhappy man that next day, when the sun was high, he would be sent with all speed to the land of shadows.

That night, the medicine man climbed to the top of a high hill in search of advice from friendly spirits on how to cover the entire earth with leather. He slept, and in a dream vision he was shown the answer to his problem. Amid vivid flashes of lightning, he tore down the steep hillside, howling louder than the big chief at times, as jagged rocks wounded his bare feet and legs. He did not stop until he was safely inside his lodge. He worked all night and until the warriors who were to send him on the shadow trail came for him, just before noon the next day. He was surrounded by the war-club armed guards. He was clutching close to his heart something tightly rolled in a piece of deerskin. His cheerful smile surprised those who saw him pass. "Wah, he is brave!" said the men of the tribe. "He is very brave!" said the women of the tribe.

The big chief was waiting just outside his lodge. He gave the guards swift, stern orders. Before the maker of magic could be led away, he asked leave to say a few words to the chief. "Speak!" said the chief, sorry to lose a clever medicine man who was very good at most kinds of magic. Even the chief knew that covering the entire earth with leather was an impossible task.

The medicine man quickly knelt beside the chief, unrolled the two objects which he took from his bundle and slipped one of them on each foot of the chief. The chief seemed to be wearing a pair of bear's hairless feet, instead of bare feet, and he was puzzled at first as he looked at the elkhide handcraft of his medicine man. "Big chief," the medicine man exclaimed joyfully, "I have found the way to cover the earth with leather! For you, O chief, from now on the earth will always be covered with leather." And so it was.

* * *

The Great Flood
Salish

Long before missionaries ever arrived in the New World, the Indians had ancient legends of a great flood, similar to that of Noah. This is the one the Cowichan tell.

In ancient times, there were so many people in the land that they lived everywhere. Soon hunting became bad and food scarce, so that the people quarreled over hunting territories.

Even in those days, the people were skilled in making fine canoes and paddles from cedars, and clothing and baskets from their bark. In dreams their wise old men could see the future, and there came a time when they all had similar bad dreams that kept coming to them over and over again. The dreams warned of a great flood. This troubled the wise men who told each other about their dreams. They found that they all had dreamed that rain fell for such a long time, or that the river rose, causing a great flood so that all of the people were drowned. They were much afraid and called a council to hear their dreams and decide what should be done. One said that they should build a great raft by tying many canoes together. Some of the people agreed, but others laughed at the old men and their dreams.

The people who believed in the dreams worked hard building the raft. It took many moons of hard work, lashing huge cedar log canoes together with strong ropes of cedar bark. When it was completed, they tied the raft with a great rope of cedar bark to the top of Mount Cowichan by passing one end of the rope through the center of a huge stone which can still be seen there.

During the time the people were working on the raft, those who did not believe in the dreams were idle and still laughed, but they did admire the fine, solid raft when it was at last finished and floated in Cowichan Bay.

Soon after the raft was ready, huge raindrops started falling, rivers overflowed, and the valleys were flooded. Although people climbed Mount Cowichan to avoid the great flood, it too was soon under water. But those who had believed the dreams took food to the raft and they and their families climbed into it as the waters rose. They lived on the raft many days and could see nothing but water. Even the mountain tops had disappeared beneath the flood. The people became much afraid when their canoes began to flood and they prayed for help. Nothing happened for a long time; then the rain stopped.

The waters began to go down after a time, and finally the raft was grounded on top of Mount Cowichan. The huge stone anchor and heavy rope had held it safe. As the water gradually sank lower and lower, the people could see their lands, but their homes had all been swept away. The valleys and forests had been destroyed. The people went back to their old land and started to rebuild their homes.

After a long time the number of people increased, until once again the land was filled and the people started to quarrel again. This time they separated into tribes and clans, all going to different places. The storytellers say this is how people spread all over the earth.

* * *

Tail of Fire

Cowichan

So long ago that the time could not be counted by suns or moons, a band of Cowichan Indians was drying deer meat in the sun. They spoke of how good it would be if they only had a small sun to warm them when the big sun left to let darkness come. They thought that they would never get that thing because what they wanted would take much power and magic, more than even their most powerful shamans had.

As the people wished and talked, a little bird chirped loudly close by. It flew close to the people and they saw that it was a beautiful

brown bird with a bright red tail which seemed to flicker even when
the bird sat still. The bird looked down on the Indians from a branch
just over their heads.

"What do you want, little bird?" asked an old man who had
power to speak with birds.

"Nothing do I wish, Wise One, but I bring you what you wish," it
replied. "I have something which is called fire on my tail, which is hot
like a small sun. It will comfort you when the winds of winter blow,
cook your meat, and bring cheer when the sun has gone, but it must
be earned. Nothing seems good or is thought well of that comes to us
too easily. Tell your tribe to meet me here when the sun comes again
and ask each one to bring a little dry branch with pitch pine on it."

Before the people could ask why, the bird suddenly disappeared.
"We should obey the wishes of that bird," the old man counseled. "It
may bring much good fortune to us."

When the sun shone again, the people awaited the coming of the
bird. Each carried a pine branch with pitch pine on it, as they had
been told. A loud *tweet* made the people look upward. The brown
bird sat on a branch above their heads, though nobody had seen it
come. It asked in a language that all understood, "Are you ready?"

They answered, "Yes!"

"Then you must follow me, and the one who first catches up with
me will be given fire, but only if the one who does so is one who does
right, is patient, and tries hard without losing courage. Come!"

The bird flew off over rough ground and thick forest. The chase
proved too hard for many and they gave up. Over fast-flowing streams
and dangerous marshes and swamps, the bird flew. More and more of

the people had neither the strength nor courage to keep on and they were forced to drop out of the chase. "Too hard!" "Too difficult!" "Too dangerous!" they gasped as they fell on the ground to rest.

At last one young warrior got close enough to call to the bird, "Give me of your fire, little bird. I have followed you far and well and I have done no wrong."

"It is not as you say," said the bird, flying higher and faster than before. "You think only of yourself. That is bad. You shall not have my fire."

A second young man caught up with the bird. "Share your fire with me," he called. "I am a good man."

"A good man does not take that which belongs to another," the bird answered, flying faster and faster. Soon, seeing it was no longer followed, the bird flew to the ground and perched beside a woman who was nursing an old man who looked very sick. "Bring a dry branch with pitch pine on it," said the brown bird. "Fire have I on my tail and you shall have it. It will keep your sick man warm and cook your food."

The woman was afraid of a bird that could speak. When she found her voice, she said, "You are good, little one, but I deserve not a magic gift. What I do, I do because it is right. The inner voice tells me that I must take care of one who is sick."

"Much good I know you do," said the bird, "and it is greater good than that done by many people because the good you do, you think is only your duty. Come, bring a branch and take of my fire. You think first of others, so you may share the gift with them."

The woman gladly brought a branch and lit it at the little fire which flickered on the bird's tail. Since that time, the Indians have had fire.

✳   ✳   ✳

How Rabbit Lost His Tail

Micmac

Long, long ago, Glooscap created all of the animals which were friendly to him and the people of the Micmac. The animals could talk like humans and they had a common language. They all did their best to help Glooscap in his work and they all had special duties. Rabbit was one of the most faithful. He was very gentle and very handsome, with thick brown fur and a long bushy tail like that of a fox. His legs were very long, and he walked like the other animals. He was chosen by Glooscap as his forest guide, so Rabbit became known as scout of the woods. Glooscap gave him special guide power so that he could guide both people and animals, no matter where they wished to go.

One sunny day in spring, after Rabbit had been away in the

woods and forest on a long scouting mission, he was very tired and sat resting on a log in the forest. His bushy tail trailed behind him. As Rabbit sat resting, an Indian who appeared to be very, very tired by long travel threw himself down near Rabbit and began to weep. Rabbit, who was so kind of heart that he could not bear to see anyone suffer, asked him why he wept. The Indian told him that he was on his way to marry a beautiful girl. Now he was lost in the forest and he was afraid that if he did not arrive in time for his wedding, which was to be that afternoon, his bride-to-be might marry a wicked forest spirit who was also in love with her.

Rabbit told the Indian to have no fear, since Rabbit was the forest guide of Glooscap. He would guide the man to the village, where the wedding was to take place, in good time. The Indian was very grateful for this promise and he and Rabbit talked together and became good friends.

As soon as the man had rested and was able to travel, they started out. Rabbit led the way, but he was so quick and nimble that he often got far in advance of his Indian friend. As he stumbled slowly on his trail, the Indian saw only a glimpse of the brown coat of his friend. At last he fell into a deep pit and was too weak to climb out. He shouted for Rabbit who came back to the pit. Since he could not reach the fallen Indian, Rabbit put his long, bushy tail down into the pit and told the Indian to hang onto it so that he could be pulled out of the deep hole. The man did as he was told, and Rabbit leaped forward, thinking to pull the Indian out, but the man was too heavy. The tail of Rabbit broke off and the man fell back into the pit, still grasping a long piece of Rabbit's tail.

Rabbit was determined not to fail. He forgot about his tail, held onto a sapling close to the pit and lowered his hind legs into it. He told the man to grasp them strongly; then Rabbit tugged and pulled so hard and his legs were stretched so much that he feared they might snap off, like his tail. They did not, but when the man was finally pulled from the pit, Rabbit's legs and his body too were stretched so much that he had to hop instead of walk. He went more slowly now, and the man followed with more caution than before.

At last, they arrived at the village where the wedding was going to take place and the people were waiting for the husband-to-be. He had arrived just in time, because the wicked forest spirit had had a long talk with the girl, while they were waiting for the groom to arrive, and had again asked her to marry him. The Indian was so grateful to Rabbit that he invited the forest guide to the ceremony, which was followed by a big feast and dance. Rabbit brushed his coat against some low bushes and put a bracelet round his neck and rings on his heels, for that was the custom, and he joined gladly in the festivities.

Some small streams ran through the forest floor where the people danced, and as the girl danced with Rabbit she nearly fell into a stream. The foot of her dress got wet and when she came out into the sun, the dress began to shrink. At first it shrank only a little, but then it shrank more and more until the skirt only reached her knees. The girl was so ashamed that Rabbit ran back into the forest to get a deerskin which was hidden in a cache there. After he had made the dress longer, he started to tie it on with a buckskin thong. He twisted the thong and held one end between his forepaws, while he held the other end between his big front teeth. He was holding the twisted cord so tightly that when a dancing couple bumped into him, the cord snapped and split his upper lip as far as his nose.

Rabbit was very calm by nature and did not complain. When he at last managed to fix the dress, he and the girl danced all evening, until her husband came to claim her when the moon was high in the sky. The Indian wanted to pay Rabbit for his services as guide but Rabbit would not take any payment, so the bride gave him a fine white fur coat to wear in winter. Rabbit was very pleased with his present and thanked her for her kindness. Because it was the color of the snows of winter, it gave Rabbit a protective color which made him almost invisible when the snows fell. He was glad because his enemies could not see him then. He wore his old brown coat in the other months.

Rabbit felt ashamed to go back to his people looking so different than when they last saw him, several moons ago. He took his time and thought of what he could say when he got back. When at last he reached home, the other rabbits were amazed at the change in his appearance, and some even laughed as they saw his tail and lip. The Rabbit people asked him where he had been. He told them that he had been far away in a country which none of them had seen or heard of. When he was asked how he lost his tail, he said that in the country where he had stayed, the people either wore their tails very short or wore none at all. Because of this, and to be in fashion, he had shortened his tail to match theirs. They asked why his waist had become so slim, and he replied that it was not fashionable there to be fat, so he had eaten less in order to become slender. Asked why he hopped instead of walked, as he used to do, he said that it was considered more fashionable to hop and so, after much practice, he had learned to move in that way. Finally they asked him why his upper lip was split. This, Rabbit explained, had happened because the strangers with whom he had stayed used knives to cut their food and sometimes to eat with. He explained that it was very difficult to eat in that way and one day he had been careless and split his lip with a sharp flint blade.

The listeners envied Rabbit, whom they believed had spoken the truth. Because of this, they copied him, so that even today his descendants look just like him—all because of an accident on the trail and another at the wedding party.

* * *

The Flying Chain

Northwest Coast

The Indian lands of the Northwest Coast are cut by great rivers and fiords, and the ocean into which they empty is dotted with hundreds of islands of all sizes. An old shaman storyteller accounts for some of these islands in the following tale.

One day a huge bird flew high above the village. The people were surprised at its size. Some said that it was a giant eagle, while others cried out that it was a thunderbird, the great bird of Indian legend which brought good, and sometimes bad, to the Indians of that territory. Some of the men of the village wanted to shoot it, so that they could get its down for ceremonies and feathers for fletching their best arrows. The old medicine man warned the people against harming the great bird, should it come within range of their arrows. It must be a bird of great magic power, he thought.

People mocked the wise old man behind his back, and watched with amazement as the great bird glided from high in the sky to soar on motionless wings over the village. The village chief had sent a fast runner to bring the clan's best hunter back to the village. He had been hunting up-river but now he joined the chief, who asked him to bring down the great bird. The hunter fitted an arrow on his bowstring and took aim. Then he lowered his bow. "Perhaps it is bad medicine that I shoot this strange bird," he muttered.

The medicine man went to the hunter and warned him against even trying to kill the mystery bird. Then, sensing that his warning might not be heeded, the medicine man hurried to his house and put on his beautiful ceremonial clothing. He put on his carved cedar headdress, decorated with ermine skins and sea lion bristles, and inlaid with gleaming abalone shells. He wrapped his goat's-wool blanket, ornamented with striking designs, around his shoulders. Then he took up his magic rattle, carved in the form of a sea bird, and hurried back to the village. A feeling of despair filled him, since he feared to be too late to prevent a tragedy.

In the old man's absence, the bird had circled the village within easy bowshot and the hunter had taken aim several times, without loosing an arrow. At last, shouts of encouragement and jeers from some of the villagers made the hunter decide to shoot. His arrow flew skyward and the great bird seemed to watch it coming. It stopped for a moment in flight, and the arrow went harmlessly past. Then all of the men and boys in the village shot many arrows at the bird without striking it even once.

Then the medicine man pushed his way into the middle of the villagers and begged them to stop shooting. He shook his rattle and sang a magic song, in the hope of making the bird fly away. The bird remained motionless for a moment. Those below could hear the slight rustling of its feathers in the breeze.

Suddenly, quick as a thunderbolt the bird dived with a shrill, deafening shriek into the group of terrified villagers. It seized the hunter by the scalp with its fierce talons and rose slowly, carrying the hunter with it. The hunter kicked his legs wildly but could not break the bird's hold. A man who had stood next to the hunter grabbed him by the ankles, in the hope of holding the bird down. Once again the wing beats of the bird started to carry it slowly upward. The old medicine man felt that he must act; so, in the hope of saving the two men, he gripped the ankles of the second man and hung on.

In a moment, the medicine man felt his feet being raised from the ground and found also that he could not open his hands to let go. Then the men and boys in the crowd seemed to lose their fear and their wits. One after another, they hitched onto the flying chain and were borne steadily upward, all of them powerless to release their grips.

The huge bird flew higher and higher, the chain of men hanging beneath it like a gigantic tail of a kite. Slowly the mystery bird winged its way over the ocean, as the fearful women and girls watched. Then a great sound of thunder filled the air, and the thunderbird loosed its talons which had held the hunter prisoner. At the same instant, the spell was broken and the great chain broke into links, each link a man or boy, who dropped like stones into the ocean. Some fell close to their village, others fell farther away. As soon as he touched the water, each villager became an island, some big and some small, but forever islands.

Even today the villagers paddle their canoes between islands which were once humans who defied the thunderbird.

* * *

Why the Moon Has Shadows

Swampy Cree

Many, many moons ago, in the forest land of the Swampy Cree, there lived a man known as Chukkapas, which meant "One-low-in-the-water." This name had been earned by him because he nearly always had his canoe overloaded, so that it rode low in the water. One day, Chukkapas and his wife were killed by a bear. Wesukechak, which in Cree means "Bitter Spirit," was a powerful wonderworker, a worker of bad as well as of good, on and for animals. He knew of the death of Chukkapas and told his two children, a boy and a girl, of the death of their parents. Bitter Spirit instructed the boy, who was younger than his sister, always to follow his sister's advice because she was wise. But the boy only laughed and did not promise, because he thought that he was now a man. The wonderworker gave the boy the name of his father. The boy was proud of his new name and he made a strong bow and some arrows and told his sister that he was going on a hunt.

"O brother, do not do so because the bears may kill you too," she said.

The boy promised not to go, but he went just as soon as his sister's back was turned. He met two bears who asked, "Do you want to fight bears?"

The boy said, "Yes."

The bears said, "See that tree? It is as strong as a bear."

Then Chukkapas shot an arrow at the tree which split in two.

The bears said, "See that stone? It is as strong as a bear."

The boy shot again, and the stone split.

This frightened the bears and they ran, but the boy followed and killed them both. When he got back to the lodge, his sister asked, "Where have you been?"

Her bother answered, "I have been in the forest where I killed two bears."

His sister was afraid for the safety of her brother, and angry too. She told Bitter Spirit, who had become a sort of guardian for the two orphans, and he also was angry, but pardoned the boy when he promised not to disobey his sister again.

But the boy spoke falsely, because he did disobey his sister again and had adventures in the forest with giant men and women and giant beavers. Because he was clever enough to escape from them, he became proud and fancied that he had become a great warrior. Bitter Spirit scolded the boy again and told him that he would disobey his sister once too often.

His sister warned the boy never to look on the moon when it was round, since strange and terrible things could happen if he did so. "The moon is too far away to harm me," the boy thought, and he laughed at the fears of his sister.

One night when the moon was full and shining brightly, the sister of Chukkapas gave him a kettle made of birchbark so that he could bring some water from the lake. He saw how bright the moon was and thought that its reflection in the calm water of the lake dared him to look at it. Chukkapas was a very foolish boy who always accepted a dare. He raised his head and stared hard at the moon. It seemed to grow brighter and bigger, and still brighter, and it seemed to call to him. Then suddenly the boy found himself high in the sky and moving upward. He cried out in terror and his voice was so loud that his sister heard it. She ran out of her spruce-bark tepee to try to help him, but she was too late. She could just see her brother disappear high in the air.

The boy's sister ran in terror to the lodge of Bitter Spirit, but even that man of magic could do nothing to help. "Your brother has broken his promise once too often," he said sadly. "Even my magic has no power to help him now."

Chukkapas was drawn onto the moon and became its prisoner forever. Even today, you can see him standing on the moon holding the kettle which he had taken to the lake.

✳ ✳ ✳

The Hermit Thrush

Iroquois

In the beginning, the birds had no song. Only man sang and each morning, as the sun came, the men of the Iroquois would greet it with a song. The birds often stopped in their flight to listen, and wished that they too could sing. One day, the Great Spirit came to earth to visit the many things which he had created. As he walked in field and forest, he found things good, but still there appeared to be something lacking.

As the Great Spirit pondered and the sun sank behind the hills in the west, he heard the musical throb of an Indian drum beaten in time to the singing of the sacred sunset song of the Iroquois. As the Great Spirit listened, he noticed that the birds appeared to be listening too. Then the great thought came to him. "That is what is missing!" he exclaimed. "The birds too should sing."

Next day, when the sun had come, the Great Spirit called a great council of all the birds. The sun was hidden by the flight of so many birds. They perched on the trees and bushes surrounding the council rock on which the Great Spirit waited.

When the air was filled with a great silence, the Great Spirit spoke. "I have called this council to know if you would like to sing as do my Indian people. Each can have his own song; and the songs will be sweetest for those who strive hardest, for all must work hard to possess things which are lovely. Do you wish for song?"

The excited twittering of the great chorus of birds as they said "Oh yes!" pleased the Great Spirit.

"So be it. Tomorrow, when the sun rises in the east, you will all fly high into the sky. Each one of you will fly as high as you can possibly fly. When you reach as close to the sky as your heart and wings will carry you, you will find your songs. The bird which flies the highest will have the most beautiful song of all." With these words, the Great Spirit disappeared.

Early next morning, so early that the moon had not yet gone to let the sun come, the birds were ready for the contest. As far as one could see, there appeared no earth, no trees, no bushes—only birds. They chirped and twittered in their excitement, as they thought of the great gift of song which was to be theirs.

Only the little brown thrush was very sad. "How," he asked himself, "can I, with my little wings, fly high enough to earn a pretty song?" As the little bird looked about him, he saw that a great, golden eagle sat beside him. As he gazed in admiration at the huge bird, an idea came to the little thrush. Quickly he hid himself under the feathers of the fine eagle.

The great bird, excited as were all the wings of the air, neither saw nor felt the little bird which was waiting to be carried skyward by the majestic bird. "With my tirelessness and power of wing, I will be certain to win," the eagle thought.

It seemed to take forever for the great, red sun to greet the feathered throng, but the moment it appeared the sky was filled with feathered things. Their rapidly beating wings sounded like the rushing wind; and the face of the earth grew dark, as even the mighty sun rose in shadow.

Ever higher flew the birds, but soon the smaller, weaker ones began to tire and drop toward the earth. Each now had a song, though many of the smaller, low-flying birds had only a few notes. As they glided down to earth, they listened to the songs which had been given to them; and they learned their songs by singing them over and over.

When the sun was leaving to let the moon come, only a few birds still flew upward. As the sun came again, only the eagle remained aloft; but even he, great chief of all the birds, began to tire when the sun was halfway toward night. His wing beats became weaker and weaker, and his efforts to continue on upward awoke the little thrush, who had slept as the great bird which carried him flew steadily upward. Now, as the eagle started to fall from the sky, the thrush flew out from his hiding place under the feathers of the eagle; and, wonder of wonders, began to fly upward.

The angry eagle scowled at the thrush and would have followed and caught the little bird. But the eagle was too tired to rise another beat, so he had to soar downward as his little passenger flew joyously upward. The little thrush flew until he came to a break in the clouds. Fearfully, he flew through and found himself in the spirit world. There he heard a lovely song. It was so beautiful that he stayed in the spirit world until he had learned every note. Then he left and flew earthward. He was eager to get back to earth so that his feathered friends could hear and admire his beautiful song.

He had flown so high that it took a long time to return to earth; and as he dropped and soared, he began to think that he had done an unfair thing, of which he should be ashamed rather than glad. The eagle had made the song possible, and he began to fear the great bird, which he knew was very angry.

When he saw the great council rock far below, he flew more and more slowly. He knew that all of the other birds would be waiting for him; and as he dropped still lower, he saw the angry eagle glaring at him. All of the birds were very still as the thrush neared the great gathering of birds. He knew that he had cheated; and he knew that all the other birds knew it too. Instead of landing, the thrush flew off into the dense forest and hid himself deep in the bushes. He did not want to see or be seen by any of the wings of the air.

Even today, he still hides deep in the woods and rarely comes out into open country. That is why he is known as the hermit thrush. Sometimes, though he is still ashamed that he cheated to get his lovely song, he sings his sweet song from the spirit world. When he does, all other birds listen in silence while his spirit song fills the air with its loveliness.

✳ ✳ ✳

Rabbit, Fire Dancer

Creek

Many a legend about Rabbit, the trickster, is told by the Creek story tellers. In some of the legends about his adventures and antics, he reminds the listeners of Raven, the trickster of the Pacific Northwest Coast Indians. In the tale which follows, Rabbit was in search of fire, as was Raven in one of his adventures.

Of course, Rabbit was one of the first on the square, on the day when the Sky people celebrated the great Green Corn Festival. During the dance, they would renew the fire, which flickered between the sacred fire logs. The dancing place was the only place where the chiefs and medicine men allowed fire to burn. The first people had no fire and wanted it very much, though they were not allowed to have it.

Rabbit believed that the Hitchiti people should have the great blessing of fire. He thought very hard on the day of the great dance. He had his friends rub his head with pitch pine until every hair on his head pointed straight up into the sky. The people thought that his crest was so wonderful that they had the chief of the ceremony appoint Rabbit as the leader of the dance. The chief and the people had seen Rabbit caper and dance before, and they knew nobody else who could put so much movement and spirit into the special dance steps.

Rabbit smiled slyly when he was made dance leader, not only because he was a natural show-off, but also for a very special reason which took all of his courage even to think about.

Bearing offerings to throw into the fire, the dancers followed capering Rabbit in the four directions shown by the logs of the fire. They thought they had never seen him dance so hard and well. He leaped high in the air, and bowed very low to the ground, as he led the circle of dancers around the low-burning fire.

On the fourth time of circling the fire, the dancers saw that Rabbit was preparing to throw the tobacco offering into the fire. The dancers knew that this would renew the fire and the Sky People would be glad when it burst into new life and flame. The leaping flame blazed far higher than the people had ever seen it burn before. This was because Rabbit had purposely thrust his pine-drenched hair into the flame, which set it ablaze. Before the medicine men or chiefs could stop or catch him, Rabbit leapt from the great square and ran fast into the nearby woods.

The angry medicine men worked great magic and caused a terrible rain which lasted for four days and four nights, and drenched all of the people. Rabbit, however, had bolted into a big, hollow tree, where he built a fine fire. When the sun shone again, he brought a blazing torch out. Once more the medicine men made a heavy rain. Even some of the people helped him with their thoughts, though they feared to have anything which the medicine men and chiefs did not want them to have.

Rabbit tried to make fires and give fire to the first people. He would not have been able to do so, had not the first people been quick to light dry branches in some of the fires. The rains kept putting out nearly all of his fires, and if they had, the first people might never have had fire. But soon, so many of these people had fire that there was always someone to give fire when the fire of another went out.

At last, the medicine men admitted that Rabbit had beaten them, and they gave up causing rain to fall in the hope of putting out the many fires. So everybody was given the right to have the blessing of fire, and the first people praised Rabbit as the hero who had brought fire to the Hitchiti.

* * *

Why the Weasel Is Nervous

Swampy Cree

The weasel, Sihkooseu, once played a bad trick on the Bitter Spirit, Wesukechak. That is why they are not friends.

The important chief Bright Nose, Wastasekoot, of the Swampy Cree tribe, had a lovely daughter who was admired by many chiefs who wished to marry her. Though she loved one of the chiefs, her father decided to hold a council and the first chief to guess her secret name could marry her. She agreed because she thought that the only one who knew her name was the one she loved.

Bitter Spirit decided to enter the contest with everyone else. Since he did not know her name, he made a plan to discover it. He went to the old net maker, the spider, and asked him to call on the girl and, by some trick, discover her name. Spider agreed. He climbed a tall tree, spun a long thread, and floated on it until he neared the camp of the chief with the beautiful daughter. Then he floated down onto the top of the chief's wigwam, peeped down, and saw the father and daughter talking about the contest, and heard the chief whisper to his daughter, "Nobody will ever guess that your secret name is For-ever-and-ever." In this way, the Spider discovered her name. He was very pleased with himself at learning this so soon, and set off to tell his friend.

Spider walked many days through the forest because there was no suitable flying wind. He began to worry that he would arrive back too late. Then he saw the weasel and begged his help. He asked Weasel to hurry and tell Bitter Spirit the girl's secret name and Weasel agreed. But as Weasel started running, he began to think things over and decided to use the information for himself instead of telling it to Bitter Spirit as he had promised. The more he thought about this, the more he liked the idea.

Weasel went to the chief's camp when the guessing contest was being held. One by one, the guessers failed. Since the girl's suitor knew her secret name, he felt safe and did not go early, so Weasel was there before him. When Weasel's turn came, he told the chief that the girl's name was For-ever-and-ever. The chief was amazed and the daughter fainted. Being honorable, the chief accepted Weasel as his son-in-law-to-be and set the date for the marriage. Weasel was very happy, so happy that he forgot about his mean trick.

The spider finally reached home and asked Bitter Spirit when his wedding was to take place. Bitter Spirit replied that he did not go to the council, since he did not have the name in time, but he had heard that Weasel had won the girl.

Spider was very angry and told Bitter Spirit what really had happened. Bitter Spirit became very angry and told the girl's father about it. Then the chief became angry with Spider for listening and with Weasel for his trick. He decided that they were all at fault and his daughter could choose for herself. The happy girl did so.

Weasel heard that he was to be punished, so he ran away. He ran and ran. Even today, he stops and listens and trembles, as though Bitter Spirit is still chasing him.

* * *

How Dogs Came to the Indians

Ojibwa

Two Ojibwa Indians in a canoe had been blown far from shore by a great wind. They had gone far and were hungry and lost. They had little strength left to paddle, so they drifted before the wind. At last, their canoe was blown onto a beach and they were glad, but not for long. Looking for the tracks of animals, they saw some huge footprints which they knew must be those of a giant. They were afraid and hid in the bushes. As they crouched low, a big arrow thudded into the ground close beside them. Then a huge giant came toward them. A caribou hung from his belt, but the man was so big that it looked like a rabbit. He told them that he did not hurt people and he liked to be a friend to little people, who seemed to the giant to be so helpless.

He asked the two lost Indians to come home with him, and since they had no food and their weapons had been lost in the storm at sea, they were glad to go with him. An evil Windigo spirit came to the lodge of the giant and told the two men that the giant had other men hidden away in the forest because he liked to eat them. The Windigo pretended to be a friend, but he was the one who wanted the men because he was an eater of people. The Windigo became very angry when the giant would not give him the two men, and finally the giant became angry too. He took a big stick and turned over a big bowl with it. A strange animal which the Indians had never seen before lay on the floor, looking up at them. It looked like a wolf to them, but the giant called the animal "Dog." The giant told him to kill the evil

Windigo spirit. The beast sprang to its feet, shook himself, and started to grow, and grow, and grow. The more he shook himself, the more he grew and the fiercer he became. He sprang at the Windigo and killed him; then the dog grew smaller and smaller and crept under the bowl.

The giant saw that the Indians were much surprised and pleased with Dog and said that he would give it to them, though it was his pet. He told the men that he would command Dog to take them home. They had no idea how this could be done, though they had seen that the giant was a maker of magic, but they thanked the friendly giant for his great gift. The giant took the men and the dog to the seashore and gave the dog a command. At once it began to grow bigger and bigger, until it was nearly as big as a horse. The giant put the two men onto the back of the dog and told them to hold on very tightly. As Dog ran into the sea, he grew still bigger and when the water was deep enough he started to swim strongly away from shore.

After a very long time, the two Ojibwa began to see a part of the seacoast which they knew, and soon the dog headed for shore. As he neared the beach, he became smaller and smaller so that the Indians had to swim for the last part of their journey. The dog left them close to their lodges and disappeared into the forest. When the men told their tribe of their adventure, the people thought that the men were speaking falsely. "Show us even the little mystery animal, Dog, and we shall believe you," a chief said.

A few moons came and went and then, one morning while the tribe slept, the dog returned to the two men. It allowed them to pet it and took food from their hands. The tribe was very much surprised to see this new creature. It stayed with the tribe.

That, as the Indians tell, was how the first dog came to the earth.

* * *

Why the Mouse Is So Silky

Swampy Cree

One day, on his wanderings in the land of the Swampy Cree, Wesuke-chak, known as Bitter Spirit, saw a big, round stone lying beside the rocky path. Because Bitter Spirit could talk and understand the lan-

guage of nature, he always spoke to the birds and beasts and many other things. Now he spoke to the stone. "Can you run fast?" he asked.

"Oh, yes," answered the stone. "Once I get started, I can run very fast."

"Good!" Bitter Spirit cried. "Then you must race me."

"I will," answered the stone, "if you can push me to where I can start."

With great difficulty, the maker of magic did so, and without waiting, the stone started to roll downhill, going faster and faster.

Wesukechak caught up with it almost at ground level and mocked it as he ran past. "You are a turtle," he laughed. "You cannot travel fast."

The stone was very angry but did not reply.

Bitter Spirit ran and ran until he was so tired that he fell down on his face and slept soundly. The stone caught up with him at last and rolled up his legs and then onto his back, where it was stopped by his shoulders. It could roll no further. Being a big and very heavy stone, it held Bitter Spirit on the ground so that he could not move. The maker of magic had awakened in pain when the stone rolled onto his legs but he could not escape in time. "Roll off my back, stone," he shouted angrily. "You are heavy; I hurt, and I cannot move."

"You mocked me when you passed me," said the stone, "but you see I have caught up with you. Now that I have stopped, I cannot move until someone sets me rolling again. I must stay here."

For many, many moons, the stone rested on the back of Bitter

Spirit and the maker of magic could not help himself to get free. At last, Thunder decided to send some of his bolts of lightning to smash the stone and set Bitter Spirit free.

"And so, O stone, you are punished for holding me here so long," cried the wondermaker as he continued on his way.

His clothes had been torn and worn, so Bitter Spirit threw them into a bark lodge which he saw nearby, ordering that they be mended. They were thrown outside so quickly and had been so well repaired that Bitter Spirit cried out in surprise. "Who are you in that lodge? Come out, so that I may see and reward you."

The maker of magic was much surprised when he saw a little mouse creep out of the lodge. It was an ugly, fat, rough-haired little creature in those days, with a short, stubby nose.

Bitter Spirit picked the mouse up very gently and stroked its little blunt nose until it became pointed. "Now you will be able to smell out your food better," he said.

Next he brushed and combed its rough hair with his fingers until the hairs of the little creature became soft as down and smooth as the fur of an otter. "Now you will be able to run more easily into little holes in tree trunks when your enemies come," Wesukechak said, and so it was.

To this day, the mouse is soft and furry and it sniffs daintily with its long nose.

✳ ✳ ✳

The Sky Raisers
Northwest Coast

The Great Transformer had changed some of the Northwest Coast world but the Indian people did not like some of the changes. In the great stretches of country around Puget Sound, the thing the people liked least was the height of the sky. They complained because they said that it was too close to their heads. The chiefs wanted the sky to be higher because some of their people climbed to the top of high cedars and disappeared into the sky world, from which they never returned. The wise men and chiefs met in council to decide what to do.

"We can push the sky higher up, if all of the people of all of our tribes will work together," declared one of the Wise Ones.

"We must cut many long poles," said a chief.

"How will the people know when to push on the sky, so that we will all work together?" asked a young chief.

"Let us decide on a time when all and everyone will be ready," a wise man said. "Maybe one moon from now, just as the sun comes?"

"Good!" agreed those in council. "But let all people and tribes shout *Ya-hoo-oo*, as they begin to push. In all of our many languages, that means 'Raise all together.'"

"We say that when we lift our great canoes," said a Chinook chief.

So the council decided, and when the sky-raising day came, the earth shook with the loud shouted *Ya-hoooo* of all the tribes. All of the people pushed as hard as they shouted. Their mighty, massed efforts caused the sky to lift very swiftly.

Only a few hunters and whalers, who had been away a long time from their homes, did not know of the sky raising. Three hunters and their dog had chased four great elk up a mountain side, to where the earth and sky nearly met. The elk leaped into the sky world and the hunters jumped up after them. When the sky was raised, the hunters and elk were lifted with it. They were turned into stars, and they can still be seen in the sky world. The three hunters are the stars in the handle of the Great Dipper, and their dog, a very little star, stands close to the middle hunter. The four elk are the stars in the bowl of the Great Dipper.

A few other people, animals, and fish, were caught in the sky world when the sky was raised. They too were turned into stars, but the people who remained on earth were happier, and the sky has remained high overhead ever since.

Today, the Indians point out the bundles of the sky-pushing-up-poles, carved on old totem poles, as proof of this legend.

＊　＊　＊

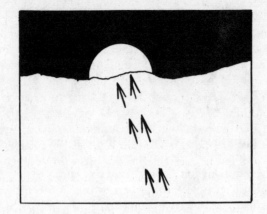

Rabbit and the Moon Man

Micmac

Long ago, Rabbit was a great hunter. He lived with his grandmother in a lodge which stood deep in the Micmac forest. It was winter and Rabbit set traps and laid snares to catch game for food. He caught many small animals and birds, until one day he discovered that some mysterious being was robbing his traps. Rabbit and his grandmother became hungry. Though he visited his traps very early each morning, he always found them empty.

At first Rabbit thought that the robber might be a cunning wolverine, until one morning he found long, narrow footprints alongside his trap line. It was, he thought, the tracks of the robber, but they looked like moonbeams. Each morning Rabbit rose earlier and earlier, but the being of the long foot was always ahead of him and always his traps were empty.

Rabbit made a trap from a bowstring with the loop so cleverly fastened that he felt certain that he would catch the robber when it came. He took one end of the thong with him and hid himself behind a clump of bushes from which he could watch his snare. It was bright moonlight while he waited, but suddenly it became very dark as the moon disappeared. A few stars were still shining and there were no clouds in the sky, so Rabbit wondered what had happened to the moon.

Someone or something came stealthily through the trees and then

Rabbit was almost blinded by a flash of bright, white light which went straight to his trap line and shone through the snare which he had set. Quick as a lightning flash, Rabbit jerked the bowstring and tightened the noose. There was a sound of struggling and the light lurched from side to side. Rabbit knew by the tugging on his string that he had caught the robber. He fastened the bowstring to a nearby sapling to hold the loop tight.

Rabbit raced back to tell his grandmother, who was a wise old woman, what had happened. She told him that he must return at once and see who or what he had caught. Rabbit, who was very frightened, wanted to wait for daylight but his grandmother said that might be too late, so he returned to his trap line.

When he came near his traps, Rabbit saw that the bright light was still there. It was so bright that it hurt his eyes. He bathed them in the icy water of a nearby brook, but still they smarted. He made big snowballs and threw them at the light, in the hope of putting it out. As they went close to the light, he heard them sizzle and saw them melt. Next, Rabbit scooped up great pawfuls of soft clay from the stream and made many big clay balls. He was a good shot and threw the balls with all of his force at the dancing white light. He heard them strike hard and then his prisoner shouted.

Then a strange, quivering voice asked why he had been snared and demanded that he be set free at once, because he was the man in the moon and he must be home before dawn came. His face had been spotted with clay and, when Rabbit went closer, the moon man saw him and threatened to kill him and all of his tribe if he were not released at once.

Rabbit was so terrified that he raced back to tell his grandmother about his strange captive. She too was much afraid and told Rabbit to return and release the thief immediately. Rabbit went back, and his voice shook with fear as he told the man in the moon that he would be released if he promised never to rob the snares again. To make doubly sure, Rabbit asked him to promise that he would never return to earth, and the moon man swore that he would never do so. Rabbit could hardly see in the dazzling light, but at last he managed to gnaw through the bowstring with his teeth and the man in the moon soon disappeared in the sky, leaving a bright trail of light behind him.

Rabbit had been nearly blinded by the great light and his shoulders were badly scorched. Even today, rabbits blink as though light is too strong for their eyes; their eyelids are pink, and their eyes water if they look at a bright light. Their lips quiver, telling of Rabbit's terror, and their shoulders appear to be scorched yellow, even in winter.

The man in the moon has never returned to earth. When he lights the world, one can still see the marks of the clay which Rabbit threw on his face. Sometimes he disappears for a few nights, when he is trying to rub the marks of the clay balls from his face. Then the world is dark; but when the man in the moon appears again, one can see that he has never been able to clean the clay marks from his shining face.

✻   ✻   ✻

Understanding Indian
Words and Phrases

Most of the North American Indian languages were picturesque and descriptive, and many of them sounded very musical as they were spoken. Because the Indians lived close to nature, a number of their names for such objects as trees, birds, animals, or stars, were an attempt to describe what they did or how they looked. Other entries in this section explain some of the common objects or actions of the Indians' daily life.

Aspen tree—the tree that whispers to itself

Big Dipper—the Seven Stars

Birds—the wings of the air

Breechclout—the loincloth worn by Indian men and boys

Coup—an honor (from the French word meaning "stroke"); to count coup meant to tell of daring feats and honors; coup feathers were specially marked feathers, often from the eagle or turkey, awarded for brave deeds and outstanding exploits.

Dark—many Indian storytellers would tell their stories only before or after dark, depending on the sort of story it was. This was for fear of offending the spirits. Thus the storytellers often started by saying, "As it is not yet dark," or "As it is now dark, I can tell my story."

217

Dark thoughts—sad or troubled thoughts

Fletch—to provide a feather for an arrow

Heart—indicated happiness or sorrow: "His heart sings" meant "He is glad", and "His heart was on the ground" meant "He was sad and discouraged."

Long house—a communal dwelling of the Iroquois and some other Indian peoples; it was usually a wooden framework covered with bark, sometimes as much as 100 feet in length.

Medicine—something of a magic nature; there was good and bad medicine.

Medicine dream—a dream in which guidance came during sleep

Months or moons—the passing of the months and years were kept track of, since some moons brought food and plenty, while others brought starvation and often death. The Blackfoot and other Indian nations and tribes had picturesque names for the months, such as February, the Hunger Moon; March, the Moon When Waterfowl Come; April, the the Green Grass Moon or the Moon When Grass Starts; May, the Moon When Trees Leaf; July, the Moon of Ripe Berries; August, the Hot Sun Moon; September, the Hunting Moon; October, the Moon of Falling Leaves; December, the Long Night Moon.

Nock—to put the arrow to the bow, in readiness to shoot

Numbers—"like the grass" meant very many.

Parfleche—dried rawhide, or an object made from it

Pemmican—dried meat pounded to a powder, often shaped into cakes

Potlatch—a huge feast given by the Indians of the Northwest Coast, at which many valuable gifts were given to the guests

Seasons—*see* Months

Shadow trail or land of shadows—the place of the dead

Speak with forked (or crooked) tongue—to tell a lie ·

Speed—terms such as "quick as an arrow" or "quick as a loon dives" were used by the Indians to describe the passing of time or the speed of fast ponies or deer.

Sun—used in telling directions: "Go toward from where the sun comes" or "Travel the path of the rising sun" meant to go east.

Tillicum—friend

Time—having only the sun, moon and stars with which to tell the passing of time, the Indians described time in ways such as these: morning was "when the sun comes"; noon was "when the sun is halfway on its journey"; night was "when the sun leaves to let the moon come"; many months were "many moons"; two days and two nights were "two suns and two sleeps"; fifteen years was called "fifteen snows" by Northern tribes; times long past were said to be "so long ago that the time cannot be counted by suns and moons"; a second was "for a heartbeat."

Totem—a sign which may represent a bird, animal, or other thing, adopted as a name or crest by a single Indian, a family, tribe or clan

Totem pole—a tall pole made from a cedar tree, set up in the ground by the Northwest Coast peoples to celebrate some important event; animals, birds, fish, spirit beings, and later family crests, were carved and painted on these "talking sticks."

Travois—two poles joined by a frame, pulled by a dog or other animal; used for transporting things.

Tyee—supernatural being; powerful spirit

Windigo—giant, evil spirit of the woods

Wise Ones—the wisest old men of the tribes; these were likely to be the chiefs, shamans, and medicine men.

Index of Tribes and Stories